APOCALYPSE LATER

ZINE
ISSUE #12

APOCALYPSE LATER BOOKS
BY HAL C. F. ASTELL

FILM

Huh? An A-Z of Why Classic American Bad Movies Were Made

Velvet Glove Cast in Iron: The Films of Tura Satana

Charlie Chaplin Centennial: Keystone

The International Horror & Sci-Fi Film Festival: The Transition Years

A Hundred in 2016

The Awesomely Awful '80s, Part 2

A Horror Movie Calendar

WTF!? Films You Won't Believe Exist

ZINE

Horns Ablaze 1-4

The Cultural References in Blazing Saddles

The First Thirty 1-2

The Library of Halexandria 1-4

APOCALYPSE LATER ZINE #12

STEAMPUNK SHORT FILMS

**THIRTY QUINTESSENTIAL STEAMPUNK
KINEMATOGRAPHS PRESENTED BY
THE APOCALYPSE LATER ROADSHOW**

BY HAL C. F. ASTELL

APOCALYPSE LATER

APOCALYPSE LATER PRESS
PHOENIX, AZ

Apocalypse Later Zine #12 — September 2023

Steampunk Short Films

ISBN-13: 978-1-961279-04-9

Apocalypse Later Press catalogue number: ALZ012

All text by Hal C. F. Astell.

Cover art generated at Wombo.

Apocalypse Later is a monthly zine published by Apocalypse Later Press.

Typeset in Cantarell, Gentium Plus, Linux Biolinum, Oswald ExtraLight, Starship Shadow Inline, Twlg Typist and Veteran Typewriter.

https://fonts.adobe.com/fonts/cantarell

https://software.sil.org/gentium/

https://sourceforge.net/projects/linuxlibertine/

https://fonts.adobe.com/fonts/oswald

https://packages.debian.org/buster/fonts-tlwg-typist-ttf

https://liveheroes.com/en/brand/typesgal

Published through Kindle Direct Publishing

https://kdp.amazon.com/

Published by Apocalypse Later Press

https://press.apocalypselaterempire.com/

ACKNOWLEDGEMENTS

Many thanks to all the filmmakers behind the films included in this zine. They kindly gave me their permission to screen their cinematic babies to audiences at Roadshow events and I literally couldn't run that show without them.

Thanks to the convention owners and programmers who keep bringing me back to their events, especially Jason Drotman at Wild Wild West Steampunk Convention, held in Tucson, Arizona, and Anastasia Hunter at Gaslight Steampunk Expo, held in San Diego, California.

Thanks also to my audience, especially the folk who come back to every Roadshow set at particular events like the two above to see what I've put together for them this year.

CONTENTS

INTRODUCTION

This was intended to be a one off film zine, but I had so much fun putting it together that I may well come back to the idea in the future.

The obvious scope is steampunk short films, because it's a genre I thoroughly enjoy and many of these films are unjustly overlooked, even within the already overlooked realm of short films. What you'll find is that many of them are longer shorts, with deep and substantial stories that are able to breathe over twenty, thirty or even forty minutes. You'll also find that many feature star names that you may not have realised had anything to do with the genre.

However, there's another scope in that I've screened every film covered in this zine in one or more of my Apocalypse Later Roadshow sets over the years, a program I've been running for just over a decade now at conventions all over the southwest. I thought it was time for a celebration.

For those who don't know what steampunk is, best of luck in finding out because every one of us probably has a different definition. One common definition is that it's Victorian science fiction and that's true to a degree, but it's also a highly limiting label.

Steampunk doesn't have to be Victorian, which would limit stories to be set between 1837 and 1901, the reign of Queen Victoria, with a heavy implication that they would unfold in England or, at least, within the British Empire. Those dates are a good guide but they're not inscribed in stone and steampunk stories can happen within any culture in the world, or indeed beyond it. Fourteen of these films are American, with four more from France, a couple from Russia, three from down under and a few from elsewhere. Only two are from the UK.

Similarly, steampunk doesn't have to be science fiction, though that's often the case because of a focus on gadgets and technology. Steampunk stories can be told in pretty much any genre with those here including horror, urban fantasy, drama, children's, romance, war, even a musical, and presented as live action or varied styles of animation, even a handful of silent films.

My take is that our world today isn't what was promised by social and technological advances a hundred and forty years ago, so we're rewinding history back to that point so we can start over, this time doing all the right things and none of the wrong ones. We can define which are which.

While my Roadshow sets are tailored to the genre and theme of any event that brings me out, I've programmed a lot at steampunk conventions. I started out in science fiction at LepreCon 39 in May 2013, but my fourth was Wild Wild West Steampunk Convention III the following March. Since then, twenty of my forty-eight shows have been dedicated to steampunk and I've seen most of what has been made up until now. If I'm missing something amazing, please let me know.

So here are thirty longer and more substantial steampunk short films that represent a variety of what the genre can do, each of which I've screened to a live audience at least once during an Apocalypse Later Roadshow set. Thank you for being there if you were. Sorry you missed it if you weren't. Fortunately, most of them can be seen online, so you can follow up by watching the ones that you missed or that pique your interest. Enjoy and maybe I'll see you at a Roadshow set soon!

1873: THE INSIDIOUS INTRIGUE (2013)

DIRECTOR: STEVE ZIOLKOWSKI

WRITER: STEVE ZIOLKOWSKI

STARS: SCOTT ANTHONY GOULD, KAT STEEL, JAMES MUSCARELLO, MARK ADAMS AND CHRIS BOWERS

One of the classic approaches for steampunk filmmakers to take is to pretend that the new film they've just created isn't new at all. This eighteen minute short is a silent movie, made just like it would have been in 1923, only half a century after the story it tells, rather than the hundred and forty years that it actually was.

It's not as easy an approach as it might seem because silent movies weren't just intertitles and overacting in compensatation for the lack of dialogue. Steve Ziolkowski, who both wrote and directed, nails the feel of the era, with the majority of the movie in sepia but some scenes colour tinted for effect. The only other recent silent films I know that are this effective are *The Unusual Inventions of Henry Cavendish* and the H. P. Lovecraft Society's *The Call of Cthulhu*.

Ziolkowski hurls us into 1873 from the very outset but it's not the 1873 we remember from history. It's a neatly visualised retro-futuristic Boston, whose airspace is alive with dirigibles and rocketships. The Boston Electroluminance Company has Tesla coils in the street to milk for power. There's an elevated steam-powered monorail in front of the Boston Aeroport. And, above it, dwarfing the building itself, is the *Hypatia*, the largest steamaeroship anywhere in the world, scheduled to depart at noon for London on its maiden flight, once humans and robotic Steamboys have finished loading it.

There's a story about to begin, but as this is only the opening chapter in a supposed series of four, the others of which were sadly never made, that story can't be our primary focus.

Instead, we revel in this vivid visualisation of a very different 1873, which, amazingly, was entirely generated on a MacBook Pro. And, if you're a film nerd like me, we marvel at how Ziolkowski visualises dialogue in a way that's at once natural and also neatly meaningful.

Dialogue in silent films is usually presented as text in intertitles, which some of it is here, but the best intertitle writers did that as little as possible, as it interrupted the visuals. It's why silent actors tended to overact, in order to get their message across physically without having to fall back onto intertitles. Ziolkowski addresses that by hurling some of the dialogue onto the screen in innovative ways.

For instance, there's a press conference on the *Hypatia* and we experience the chatter of the journalists impressionistically, because the words they say overlap, as if we're catching a glimpse here and a snatch there. These lines also overlap, some lurking in the background and some creeping into frame or popping in and out of being. They're shown in different fonts, thus hinting at different accents, and in different languages too. There are also points when the same line of dialogue is shown from the front and from behind, because we shifted character perspective and the words are like a physical thing hanging out between them. It's masterfully done.

But back to that story, because I can't ignore it entirely. Our lead appears to be Jack Mulvey, a talented young inventor who designed the *Hypatia*, which appears to be a masterpiece of engineering, even if it's just a step on the way to his real goal of flying to the Moon. While we don't spend a huge amount of time with any of these characters, Scott Anthony Gould is able to get across that Jack is a idealistic soul who's surrounded by opportunists.

One of those is Baron Glowerston, played by Ziolkowski himself. He's a wealthy tycoon type who runs the Glowerston Aeroship Dock, owns the *Hypatia* and has bargained away Fanny, his unwilling daughter, to the most overt villain of the piece, Farnsworth, for reasons we're not yet made aware. However, he's not yet aware that she's in love with Wu, his highly capable bodyguard and assassin, who has plans of his own to avoid her becoming Mrs. Farnsworth.

Everyone in this picture has plans and the insidious intrigue of the title is how they play out together. We don't really know who does what to who, for the most part, or whether the next episode will introduce new players to the game, like perhaps Impey Barbicane, president of the Baltimore Gun Club, who's also aiming for the Moon. It really doesn't matter, because all that's a big MacGuffin, What matters is that there's lots of intrigue and we're kept guessing about the next reveal before it's delivered.

Talking of MacGuffins, Glowerston has quite a serious collection of cool stuff and, just as we know that Mulvey wants to visit the Moon, we know that Glowerston wants to locate a sword called the Sisyphi Desperatio, sketched by one M. Arronax, scientist and narrator of *Twenty Thousand Leagues under the Sea*, so potentially found in the depths by Captain Nemo. We can have a level of confidence in his abilities too, as the Glowerston Artifact Collection already contains the mirror shield from *Clash of the Titans*, as well as the Ark of the Covenant from *Raiders of the Lost Ark*. Who knows what else is in those packing crates?

Well, there's a lot we don't know and we're sadly not going to be able to find out from the next three thrilling instalments of *1873*, for no better reason than they don't exist. However, there's much to enjoy from this first chapter anyway, even if it inherently doesn't finish the story that it starts.

The visuals are probably the biggest reason, both in how they were designed and how they were executed on Ziolkowski's MacBook Pro. I love the Steamboy automaton design, not just externally but also internally, given that their brains process programming through a music box cylinder. Talking of music, that's a strong aspect too, vibrant throughout courtesy of the score by Terry Michael Huud and well chosen classical works by Ravel, Holst and Stravinsky.

The acting is appropriate for a silent movie, but Chris Bowers's take on Wu is particularly memorable, his infuriatingly calm demeanour a pristine example of being centered and ever-aware of what's going on. And I believe he's a previsualisation artist not an actor, that being someone who maps out what scenes will look like before they do. He's done that on films as prominent as *Captain America*, *Rise of the Planet of the Apes* and *Alice Through the Looking Glass*.

Finally, there's the humour, which shines in the editing, as some scenes segue wonderfully into others, and the writing. Both show up in a flashback to when Jack and Fanny were kids and the former tells the latter, "Hah! You can't go to the Moon, Fanny! SCIENCE is for BOYS!" She slaps him in the flashback and present day in one fell swoop. SPACK! indeed.

THE ANACHRONISM (2008)

DIRECTOR: MATTHEW GORDON LONG
WRITER: MATTHEW GORDON LONG
STARS: KATARINA WATT AND RYAN GRANTHAM

Steampunk is inherently speculative fiction and a classic genre approach to telling a story is to begin as a drama, then change something in an impossible or unprecedented way to see what happens. Here's a great example.

Katie and Sebastian are children who fancy themselves amateur scientists. This short film was shot in British Columbia so we can assume that the characters live there as well, merely a century and change ago, based on what little evidence we can muster, as Matthew Gordon Long, who wrote and directed, doesn't tell us anything for sure and we can read things in at least a couple of different ways.

The beautiful landscape is lush, green and coastal. Their clothing is old fashioned, from our way of thinking, as are the accoutrements they take with them: a parasol, a butterfly net and a scientific reference book packed full of detailed engravings. Vancouver was founded in 1870, as Granville, so it seems fair to see this as late in the nineteenth century on the west coast of Canada. It doesn't matter, of course. It would be enough to accept it as the past.

They use these accoutrements on scientific expeditions, as they wander about the woods, take impressions of what they find in a journal using prints or rubbings, then classify them in accordance with the taxonomic system. That's true whether they're recording bugs, plants or even Sebastian himself.

They're pretty good at taxonomy for kids, a detail I appreciated because I used to do much the same when I was a kid, merely drawing the insects I found in the garden, then attempting to identify them with the aid of a much more modern and colourful pocket reference.

However, they're stuck when they stumble upon a mechanical squid on the beach. That's the anachronism of the title, that and whoever they find inside it that they accidentally free from its metal clutches. Kingdom: "Animalia." Phylum? "Mollusca. I think." Class? That must be "Unknown."

There's an old show business maxim that we should never work with children or animals. It wasn't followed by Long, who cast a couple of child actors as his leads, adding a third inside this device, which is made of metal and so isn't a living creature at all, and relegating the one and only adult in the film to the bookends.

However, he cast well, at least as far as he could know at the time. Katarina Watt is very good as Katie, believably precocious for a girl in the Victorian era who's still young enough not to be talked out of it, but also capable of a combination of insight, panic and toughness. It has to be said that she's the brave one of the pair, even if her younger brother musters up a modicum of courage when needs must. This is her only credit in IMDb.

That younger brother, Sebastian, is played by an actor who absolutely did go somewhere, initially into a lot of impressive credits on TV and in film but eventually also into prison. He was busy when he made this short, following up with roles in movies like *The Imaginarium of Doctor Parnassus* and *Diary of a Wimpy Kid* and a string of episodes for TV shows like *iZombie* and *Supernatural*. He certainly had promise.

Sadly, he then shot his mum in the back of the head rather than admit to her that he had planned and given up on a plan to assassinate the Canadian prime minister, Justin Trudeau, and possibly follow up with a mass shooting at a local university. That was 2020 when he was 21 and he got an automatic life sentence. He'll not be eligible for parole until at least 2036.

It's hard to imagine the little kid in this film as a future murderer but then again Sebastian does make some poor choices here. It's he who loses the parasol by poking it into a hole in the side of the squid, at which point it eats it. It's he who removes the breathing apparatus from the creature inside the squid too, apparently not considering that it might not breathe the same air that we do. Whether this young lady was already dead before that point or not, she certainly is afterwards.

What's interesting here isn't just that there happens to be a humanoid creature inside this mechanical squid, it's also that the craft, as we must consider it, has a plaque mounted to its outer shell, one that we recognise because it's very similar to the one that was famously sent out into the stars on board *Pioneer* 10 and 11. You know the one. Carl Sagan designed it and it's been a pop culture staple ever since. It just didn't have a squid for a spaceship.

What's great about this whole setup is that it prompts us to be amateur scientists just like Katie and Sebastian. We're well over a century more advanced technologically than them, so how should we apply what we know to what

they found?

If this squid is a ship, then when and where has it come from? How does it work? We're in an otherwise Victorian setting, so is this really a time machine and this young lady has gone back in time? If so, why? What's happening in her future for her to need to go back? It seems unlikely to be a ship for travelling in space, so could it have come from a parallel dimension? That happens a lot in science fiction nowadays and in superhero stories too. Has it travelled through a rift in the time/space continuum to our universe? After all, we don't design ships like squid, even in Japan. Or did it originate in our world and travel elsewhere? Maybe it's a vehicle to move through both time and space like a TARDIS.

The bottom line is that we don't know and it doesn't matter how many times we watch this short, Long didn't leave enough clues here for us to find those answers. We have to come up with our own from our own deduction and our own intuition. This mechanical squid is a great anachronism and a great MacGuffin.

I just wish I knew more about it. Long made four films, IMDb tells me this being the third of them and the only one I've seen. The others don't appear to resemble this one much at all, but maybe they do. *The Great Retro-Chic Revival* features a future society of drones thawing a cryogenically frozen human being from 1987, so may be this story in reverse. *Lillian Code* is a period piece that follows a Russian woman on a solo walk from New York to Siberia in 1928, so another story starring a driven woman who was presumably an anachronism at one end of her walk, at least, possibly both.

However, I've never been able to reach him. I hope he's alive and well and enjoying life and aware that people still enjoy this film.

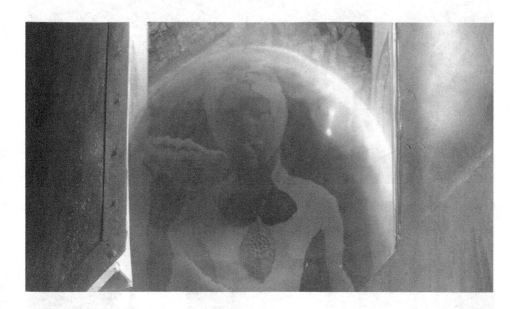

BILL & MAGGIE'S INTERGALACTIC TAXI SERVICE (2017)

DIRECTOR: JONATHAN LEITER

WRITER: JONATHAN LEITER

STARS: TIMMY GIBSON, COURTNEY FORTNER, NORA LAIDMAN, TYLER LINKE, MICHAEL BUNCH AND ARIC BUNCH

Bill & Maggie's Intergalactic Taxi Service starts out with the exact same approach as *1873: The Insidious Intrigue*: tell a futuristic story through the medium of history, as a silent film, shot in sepia in a 4:3 aspect ratio. It even uses a clever way to handle dialogue, by popping up speech bubbles like this is an animated comic book.

However, it doesn't stay there, choosing to explode into colour and widescreen instead as the *Chimera*, the taxi of the title, hurtles its way through space on its way to the sovereign world of Pluto to deliver Her Majesty, Queen Victoria IV to a bi-annual International United Planets Conference.

The reason for this is pretty cool. The plan is for William Sprocket, captain of the *Chimera*, to fly her there, if that's the right term to use for a space taxi that looks rather like a sailing ship, at which point the entire voyage would be boringly routine, hence sepia.

However, a disagreement over the contract —which is annoyingly not the suggestion that the British Empire in 2546 has switched to the idiotic mm/dd/yyyy American date format— has Capt. Sprocket bicker with Lord Sheldon, Her Majesty's Royal Councel (sic), long enough for the Queen to wander on board; pick up the key that makes the ship go, from the floor; and hand it to Maggie, the captain's daughter, who is aching to fly the taxi for the first time. And, suddenly, everything comes alive for Maggie and we switch to vibrant colour to reflect that.

The film remains silent, with certain sound effects, but that's fine. Dialogue here wouldn't help the story, which is told more through the time honoured art of slapstick than words. It works impeccably, given the film's irreverent sense of humour. Sure, it's extremely silly, but I doubt anyone watching will fail to recognise John Cleese in Tyler Linke's approach to Lord Thaddeus Sheldon, so we're well prepared for this to be *Monty Python* tackling steampunk.

It isn't, because it's far more gentle than it is anarchic, but there's certainly surreality here. Once the *Chimera* takes off, Sprocket, Sheldon and the two guards accompanying him, grab a nearby vessel and give pursuit, as we'd expect, but that nearby vessel turns out to be a space age VW bus. It also doesn't corner very well in the stereotypical asteroid navigation scene, so these four characters mimic gravity effects in their cramped quarters, as if it was the bridge of the *Enterprise* being pummelled by Klingons.

I adored those scenes, as outrageously silly as they are, and I'm clearly not alone, based on the reaction of the audience when I screened it in the Roadshow. I pictured Jonathan Leiter, the writer and director, waving his arms at his cast to say "Lean that way! Now this way! Now forward! Now up! You're being sucked down a volcano!" and they all follow suit as best they can, while standing in front of a greenscreen.

"Now, Guard #2, barf in your helmet!"

This must have been so much fun to shoot, though I can also imagine just how long it had to have taken the effects team to add in all the backgrounds. Most of what we see here is CGI; only the bridge of the *Chimera* seems to be an actual physical set and that not a particularly expensive one. I recognise some of the props and it wouldn't shock me if some of the rest is made out of cardboard. It doesn't matter. It all works well enough and the bright CGI fills our attention most of the time anyway.

It's fortunate that the sense of fun remained in place for us to feed off because there's not a lot here otherwise, to be honest.

The plot is acutely simple, even if it's a neat subversion of Victorian gender roles. We have to recall all those ridiculous ideas about how the fairer sex couldn't travel more than forty miles per hour or their poor little brains might explode. Maggie's never flown this taxi before, though she's paid a lot of attention and taken a lot of notes. Now she's actually doing it, she's clearly just as good as her father. In fact, she's probably better, given that he manages to fly that VW space van into an asteroid, is sucked into a volcano and thrown out again on fire. It isn't pretty driving on his part.

The acting is fun and frankly all it needs to be, but it's also clearly amateur and the actors are deliberately playing into as many tropes as they can instead of avoiding them, in addition to overplaying in the silent style. I'd like to see some of these folk in other work, but few have other credits.

And don't lets try to figure out the logistics of the journey. I get that the planets aren't all lined up the way they are in textbooks, but the *Chimera* takes quite a tour of the solar system and it doesn't flow for me. Maybe that's why it

goes to warp speed and dives into a wormhole or whatever wonders Leiter conjured up with his CGI. Better not to fathom it. It looks pretty and the action plays into the humour and it's all fun. That's what matters!

The only thing I'd call out as odd is that the score by Ricardo Ochoa, which is orchestral in nature and suitably playful, stops at a couple of points in what seems like deliberate fashion but I can't see why.

The first starts when the men are grousing about the contract on the dock, so this silent movie goes truly silent when Victoria enters the ship. Every time I watch it, I wonder if I'm playing the right sound mix, but then I hear a variety of sound effects, when Victoria's foot bumps into the key on the bridge floor and as she talks to Maggie, so it's definitely working, just without a score. It kicks back in when she hands Maggie the key, which is arguably the most pivotal moment in the film.

The other comes when Capt. Sprocket crash lands the VW space bus onto Pluto, so they all get out and collapse in the dust in silence. It's only when Maggie hands the key back to her father and he and the Queen's retinue look at it in a sort of open mouthed horror that we're launched back into the score. So there must be meaning to the pauses there, but it doesn't gel for me.

Whatever the reason, this is a huge amount of fun. *1873: The Insidious Intrigue* contained an element of humour, but was a serious thriller in the serial vein. *The Anachronism* was serious drama too. This is comedy and it underlines a sense of playfulness in steampunk that's often forgotten in adaptations. It's absolutely there in the scene. Why not throw it onto the screen too? Well, that's what Jonathan Leiter did and I'm happy for it.

CORSET (2015)

DIRECTOR: OLGA TWIGHLIGHT

WRITER: OLGA TWIGHLIGHT

STARS: VADIM DEMCHOG, YURY UTKIN, YULIYA LAZERSON, IVAN OZHOGIN AND VERA SVESHNIKOVA

Some of my favourite steampunk shorts are the ones that run long and give their creators space to let their stories breathe. This runs for exactly half an hour and unfolds on the grand scale of an opera.

We're in Twighburg, the capital of a Russian empire whose aesthetics are not only rooted in steampunk but also goth culture. There are no vampires here, but it's no stretch that some of the many characters we glimpse in passing could be. Instead, the supernatural element is more occult in nature, which also fits the sets. We aren't given a year but this feels Victorian, merely also in a part of the world where much of the surroundings is far older.

For instance, Master Ferdinand's house is a castle, built out of stone that's obviously seen its share of battles. It's centuries older than we might expect for steampunk, so automatically adds privilege, but it also serves well for opera and gothic storytelling. Like everything in this film, it's gorgeous and cinematic, even if we're kept in certain small areas of it.

He's the most famous corset maker in all of Twighburg, even though he's missing an eye, and he's seeking a new assistant. Young Gloria Hutmacher, newly arrived in town from Under Neu Stadt, sees his ad in the paper after her purse is stolen at the station and won't take no for an answer.

Vadim Demchog and Juliya Lazerson are the two actors and they're both perfectly cast for this style of movie.

Master Ferdinand isn't an old man, though he might be three times Gloria's age. However, we can easily buy into him having lived for an incredibly long time, mastering his craft over centuries, but has become so focused on work that he has no connection left to the society that grew up around him. So now he lives for moments, for challenges, and has the patience to wait for them. He sees one in Gloria.

We see more than she initially presents too. She shows up at Ferdinand's castle meek and mild, seeking employment with a quiet voice, but she's no mouse. She's a lion and she finds a moment to roar even in her first meeting with the master. "I will win this town," she explains to him and she's absolutely serious.

This is a great dynamic for us and it's ready for these actors to play to. It's easy to believe Demchog dominating any scene he wants, but he enjoys doing that most with the quiet ones, even if he can also effortlessly rage as needed. Lazerson can play a cringing recipient of such anger but we always see the power within her ready to fight its way out and take over.

There are a couple of mirrored scenes here that illustrate how much she changes and how quickly. They're set on the castle stairs leading up to Master Ferdinand's rooms, early in the morning when there's a need for someone to pick up fresh produce from the market. When we see this first, Gloria is new and willing and so she shows up with a basket containing what she's been able to buy. When we return to this scene, she's accepted a deal from the master and met its terms, so she waltzes in from the night before with nothing but her fine clothes and her nose in the air, expecting Manfred, the master's impeccable servant, to handle the menial labour. She isn't a maid, she says; she's the master's assistant.

It's when that deal is set that we see where we're going, at least as far as we can. Gloria is established now and confident enough in her position to flippantly imitate the society ladies who fawned all over the master during their recent fittings. One of them, Madame Talkon, in the form of Olga Twighlight, the creator of this film and its world, laughed that his talent is sourced from a deal with the devil. We take that as mere flattery, but after Gloria's cheeky impersonations, he raises his goggles up to his blind eye and taps into something esoteric and occult. Things go red, magical symbols appear and suddenly an invitation to a society ball in a wax sealed envelope literally falls out of the air. We take Madame Talkon's words literally.

The deal is an odd one. If Gloria proves able to charm the high society, then he will make her a very special corset, one that will capture and defeat the city. This is opera, you'll recall, even if it isn't sung, so we're operating on the grandest scale and everything is superlatives. And, of course, if you know how operas end, it won't be much of a surprise where this goes.

There are all sorts of technical details that I could rave about, like the cinematography and the editing, but what struck me quickly on my first viewing, continues to strike me on every subsequent time through and I find echoed by the audiences whenever I screen it, is just how immersive this steampunk world is.

That's a combination of costuming, location scouting, production design and likely a little bit of collecting the right people over time to throw into the background, because I always had the impression that Twighlight is part of all these scenes. Boil all that up in this heady mix and Twighburg comes alive for us in ways that rarely happen in short films that started out as university diploma films and were then crowdfunded into happening.

If I'm understanding correctly, this film cost about $10,000 to make, through Planeta, which is a Russian crowdfunding site, with a further $2,000 for post-production and another $2,000 for promotion. That's presumably how it made it to San Diego Comic-Con, where a steampunk conrunner I know met Olga and passed on my contact details. Thanks, Diana!

That's not much money for a half hour film, but every scene here looks lush. We see Gloria getting off a real steam train. Every character we see is costumed impeccably. She passes a bevy of circus performers in the street. Every gate and wall and staircase looks perfect. Even the extras, whose only task is to walk past the camera, are costumed as lavishly as we might expect from the leads. It all looks glorious.

Later, that escalates with performances at society balls that include human statues, fire performers and contortionists, even a DJ who scratches twin gramophones. And to seal the tone, there's a song, a gothic rock/metal song from German electro-industrial band In Strict Confidence that fits perfectly.

It's not surprising that such an immersive world should spawn more films. This implies seven explicit sequels that haven't been made, but there is at least a broader *Twighburg Stories* webseries that can be watched online.

THE CRAFTSMAN (2014)

DIRECTOR: MARCELLO BARETTA

WRITER: MARCELLO BARETTA

STARS: WILLIAM ANGIULI, SYLVIA PERNARELLA, IRENEO GEROLOMINO AND ALESSANDRO CASU

Of course, not all steampunk films are lavish thirty minute affairs. Many are shorter, more focused stories like this one, a straightforward sweet romance from Italy that runs only seven minutes and is as exquisitely simple as it has to be to be told in so short a time.

In fact it's so simple that I'm painfully aware that I'm not remotely going to be able to talk about it for two whole pages, but that doesn't diminish its worth. *Corset* had a thirty minute story to tell and it did that wonderfully. In this case, *The Craftsman* has a seven minute story to tell and it also does that wonderfully, starting out with classic silhoutte animation and then shifting into live action.

It's a story all about "a brilliant inventor of amazing mechanical devices", as the narrator tells us, who works constantly and so has nigh on forgotten that there's a world outside that he can't see through his telescope. Except he does. He accidentally catches sight of Her and that world changes immediately. He's in love.

Naturally, a potential suitor must have a gift for the lady he woos, so he creates one. He's an inventor, after all, so he designs a set of five mechanical flowers which blossom when the sun catches a solar panel on the side, exposing the crystals within. And off he goes to deliver it to his newfound love, who doesn't yet know he even exists.

Well, it's not entirely that simple, because a romance has to have an obstacle for its lovers to overcome and we certainly bump into one of those, but it's almost that simple and so I'm not going to tell you any more about the story.

What I will say is that Marcello Baretta, the writer and director, distilled his story down to the quick and told it without embellishments. The narrator does his bit, the craftsman does his bit and the story's told, with a neat finalé that I won't spoil except to highlight that it's only at this point that the craftsman actually speaks and it wouldn't surprise me if a lot of viewers don't realise that. This is not a silent film, but the craftsman has no need of a voice until that moment. The way he communicates is through his creations which speak for him. Not giving him lines until that moment was a clever little touch that I don't believe I noticed on my first viewing.

Of course, without a voice, there's not much for actor William Anguili to do except look as if he's in love, which he does. He's well cast, as a character who ends up grounded but could easily lose that grounding at any moment if an idea struck him and he throws himself into its development. There's believable obsession in him but he also has bearing enough to own it and control it, instead of the other way round.

And, of course, nobody else really has much to do. Sylvia Pernarella is tasked with being as beautiful as a lovestruck man believes his girl to be and delivers on that front. She also has to deal with an elderly suitor clearly far older than she, but Ireneo Gerolomino has the poise and elegance not to make that creepy, merely period accurate. That leaves Alessandro Casu, a young man who arrives during that finalé to help wrap it all up. Nobody lets the side down, but only Angiuli really has anything to do.

Anything else I have to say wouldn't add to what I've already said, because every element plays into the same overall effect, that this is a short and simple romance that does precisely what it needs to do, then gets out of the way so the next film in a short film set can do what it needs to do in turn. While I could talk about Baretta's editing or the suitably light hearted score by Giacomo Maugeri, you probably don't need that. Either you've already gone to watch this online or it's not your thing.

What I will say, given that this zine is about steampunk, is that the mechanical flowers at the heart of the story are just as effective and also just as simple as the story itself, which is a neat touch. The credits tell me that they were made by Filiberto Camerini and Giuliano Testa and I dearly hope that they're craftsmen who have their own little stories to tell too.

Because it's always much easier to fit seven minute shorts into a short film set than thirty minute shorts, I've screened this a few times at different events and it's always received in the same way: everyone's happier after it ends than before it begins. Their faces light up, just like the mechanical flowers, and they forget in the moment that they're reading subtitles. It's the magic of cinema and, done right, that can be achieved by a story as simple as this one.

Incidentally, if you like the story but want it to be a little more complex, then it exists. It's called *The Unusual Inventions of Henry Cavendish*, it was made nine years earlier and it's also in this zine.

She was the most beautiful creature he had ever seen.

CREATURES OF WHITECHAPEL (2016)

DIRECTOR: JONATHAN MARTIN

WRITERS: JONATHAN AND REBECCA MARTIN

STARS: CARLEE BAKER, BARRETT OGDEN, RICK MACY, JILLIAN JOY, TONI HALLORAN, CRYSTAL UDY AND REEVE BOYD

People often ask me where I find the films that I screen and there are a lot of answers to be given. One is that some films, like *Creatures of Whitechapel*, were submitted to my full film festival, ALIFFF, which was oddly appropriate given that its director, Jonathan Martin, also runs a film festival himself, FilmQuest in Utah. I selected the film and my judges selected it as their Best Horror Short for 2017.

It's horror before it's steampunk but I get to program both in the Roadshow, possibly at the same time if the theme is right, and its brand of horror is right up the steampunk's alley, as a mashup of Mary Shelley's *Frankenstein* story with the historical Jack the Ripper murders.

And, talking of alleys, that's where we start out, in London in 1888, as a lady of the evening is followed by an admirer. Another lady. With yellow hair and tobacco-stained teeth. And an impressive straight razor that she uses to slice the girl's throat. It's luridly lit and gruesomely magnetic. She tears off a chunk with her teeth to chew and spit on the floor.

Cut to Dr. Pretorius slicing his steak, saying "Savage! Absolutely savage!" to his friend, Dr. Frankenstein, at the dinner table. This whole film is played delightfully straight but it has a strong sense of humour that hearkens back to the campness of James Whale's pivotal *Bride of Frankenstein* in 1935.

Here's where we learn that the razor lady is both Jack the Ripper and Igor, Frankenstein's assistant, all of which Dr. Pretorius knows but asks about anyway. Like the best interviewers, he knows the answers to the questions that he asks, but asks them anyway to get a response, ending with a hint. All Frankenstein needs is a heart. And the light bulb goes off.

All three of these actors shine, knowing the tone and relishing it.

Carlee Baker is the lead, as Igor and Jack, and she delights in the double role, bringing a surprising amount of depth to the former as the story grows in directions we likely don't expect. My favourite moment in the film is the scene where she picks up Catherine Eddowes, rescuing her from a john with no money. He's angered, so follows them and Igor, in a flash, has him up against a wall with a straight razor to his throat, roaring "Mine!"

Barrett Ogden is suitably driven and insane as Victor Frankenstein. "By God, she lives!" he cries in victory but then corrects himself. "No, not by God! By me!" He also takes this classic part a step further than usual into necrophilia, which we don't see but is clearly both implied and referenced. Sure, the corpse on his table is a beautiful young lady, amalgamated from the working girls Jack the Ripper has murdered, but that doesn't make it better!

By comparison, Rick Macy isn't given a lot of screen time as Dr. Pretorius but he's happy to milk every syllable of every word he has in classic fashion. He's an absolute delight with a supercilious air that's all the better because he backs it up. While Victor Frankenstein may be the overtly mad scientist here, Dr. Pretorius is his infuriatingly calm equivalent. Sure, there's madness in his eyes, but there's also a twinkle that never goes away.

I mentioned that Jonathan Martin runs his own film festival and that's important because this short is twenty-five minutes long. Anyone who programs film festivals knows that there is only ever so much room to work with and a whole slew of worthy films fighting it out for that skimpy scheduling space. Therefore, any film of this length isn't merely competing with another similar film but also with two twelve minute films and, especially with horror, four seven minute films. Such a creature has to be a better choice than all four of those to get into a festival. It's therefore telling that *Creatures of Whitechapel* did very well at film festivals.

I love everything about it, from its revisiting Victorian fiction and combining it with fact to its gleefully lurid lighting, all vibrant reds and blues and greens, rarely just whites.

I love that it isn't remotely hesitant to push the envelope, not only in its employment of a taboo as abiding as necrophilia but also in its genderbending of both Jack and Igor and the ensuing lesbian overtones that simply can't be ignored. There's one scene in particular that explicitly links sex and death, and all for the benefit of medical science.

I love the little Easter Eggs that are there for us to find if only we pay attention. Just in case we needed it after the scene with Dr. Pretorius and Dr. Frankenstein, we see Igor interrupted from writing a Yours Truly letter from Jack, in believable handwriting too. There's a mention

of gods and monsters that's neatly updated for this film. Originally, in *Bride of Frankenstein*, Dr. Pretorius toasts, "To a new world of gods and monsters!" Here, Dr. Frankenstein proclaims, "We are now gods!", and Igor replies, "There are no gods here. Only monsters." Of course, a white streak is added to the creature's hair by her resurrection too.

One detail that I can't assume is an homage but tickled my fancy anyway is the moment of doubt after Frankenstein has fit the heart of a woman in love into his monster's chest. It has been suitably jolted by lightning but it doesn't beat. Of course, it eventually does but he can't help but doubt his eyes and thus resorts to the classic task of wrestling referees faced with a wrestler in the sleeper hold. They hold up the arm of the victim to see if it stays up, which it never does until the third attempt, after which the victim can summon strength needed from the crowd to break the hold, rise to their feet and then turn the tables. If Frankenstein had waited for the third attempt, I'd buy into this being a deliberate homage, but a second is still a strong hint.

And I could just keep on going. The editing is wonderful. The pace is wonderful. The end credits are wonderful and there's even a scene waiting for us after them, which adds another gloriously subtle touch to the film that I don't believe I realised until after a few viewings.

There's a time-honoured misunderstanding about *Frankenstein* that never goes away. Who is Frankenstein and who is the monster? Now, it's not as simple as saying Frankenstein is the doctor and not the monster, because he's also the monster in deed, if not in make-up. Here, if we extrapolate to the hinted sequel that will never be made, he'll also become the Monster. I loved that final little touch too.

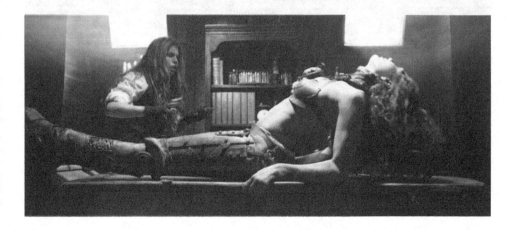

DELLA MORTIKA: CAROUSEL OF SHAME (2018)

DIRECTOR: MARISA MARTIN
WRITER: GERALDINE MARTIN
STARS: LAURA BRENT, DENA KAPLAN AND GIGI EDGLEY

While *Creatures of Whitechapel* and *Carousel of Shame* are both steampunk shorts set in 1888 created by families called Martin, they could not be more different otherwise. It's not only that the former takes place in London but the latter on the very opposite side of the globe in Melbourne, Australia. It's also that steampunk is versatile enough as a genre to veer from a taboo-breaking adult horror short to a pop-up style animation for children.

We're in Melbourne to see the Dellamorte sisters, who are English but also orphaned and so live at the Skipping Girl Home for Wayward and Homeless Girls, run by the appropriately named harridan, Mrs. Crotchett Smythe.

I'm not sure if they were created specifically for this film or whether this film was the first creative outlet they found, but there's a world beyond it that has grown to three novels and a lot more. That world was created by a mother and daughter, Geraldine Martin handling the writing and Marisa the design and animation, both of them doing great work.

Notably, it was also well publicised work, as I found the *Della Mortika* website long before it had a film to link to. I believe I bugged Marisa about progress for a few years before she was able to share the finished film and give me the permission to screen it. Now it occupies a slot in the *Della Mortika* chronology in between the second and third novels.

As children's stories often are, this is simple enough for its message to be understood on a first viewing but also deep enough to warrant further visits. It's a lot of fun too, despite the settings hinting at a darker substance. We kick off in an orphanage, which we know were not fun in Victorian times, and the carousel of the title is designed for public humiliation.

It's a fate reserved for minor criminals like pickpockets, vandals and luddites; and people deemed by polite society to display attributes that are undesirable, meaning the feckless, the indiscreet and the loquacious, each of whom is placed inside a cage which revolves in public, each with a sign telling why it's populated. I presume that the public might throw insults and maybe tomatoes.

By the way, this is an Australian film so one of those signs prompted me to look up a word, "shonky", which means unreliable. Naturally, that's been adopted by a dance DJ.

Everything's set up carefully, in adherence to the principle of Chekhov's gun, namely that every detail must have meaning for the wider story. The more times you see this, and I'm on a lot, the more succinct it seems.

What sets everything in motion is a radio-lithograph that notifies Mrs. Crotchett Smythe of an upcoming inspection on Monday, which needs to go better than its predecessor. So, she plans to give a positive impression by sending Abigail out to the marketplace to buy ribbons for the girls' hair, which sparks jealousy in her impetuous younger sister Beatrix.

After all, it's said that the soldiers will be in town today, so she wants to go too to see them and the pair, with their youngest sister Zarah, always do everything together. Mrs. Crotchett Smythe shuts her down immediately, pointing out that, unlike her elder sister who's always neatly presented, Beatrix only has a mangled mop of unruly hair on her head. Of course, that just makes it worse.

I'm sure you won't be shocked to find that Beatrix and Zarah sneak out anyway to follow Abigail into town and have an adventure. I'm sure you won't be shocked to find that Beatrix meets a soldier, dashing Lt. Pasha Dimitrikov from St. Petersburg, Russia, and promptly falls in love. And, I'm sure you won't be shocked to find the girls are caught the moment they get back to the home.

If you weren't shocked at any of those three revelations and you were paying attention to Chekhov's Gun, then you may be able to write the rest of this script yourself. However, even if you can do that, which isn't guaranteed, you would miss how well it's presented here.

Outside of traditional 2D animation, which we know from classic Disney movies, and CGI 3D animation, which we learned from Pixar, it must be said that animation is a versatile and often acutely personal thing. It's rather akin to the human voice, in that so many people use it to do similar things with thoroughly different results. Marisa Martin's style of animation is a unique voice that's immediately familiar from our childhoods and yet also refreshingly new in an animated short film.

That's because she took the template for her design from pop-up books for children, which also serve as transitions between scenes here. She hand crafted characters out of paper and articulated them with rivets, so that she could animate them with stop motion photography. It's utterly charming but also very appropriate for the Victorian era.

Just like with pop-up books, she also creates depth in her scenes by using layering, so that this bit is literally in front of that bit. She also includes the equivalent of interactive points, where we would normally pull a piece of card to make something move. Obviously, we can't do that with a short film so she does it for us, so that, say, that radio-lithograph slides out of its designated slot in a delivery box and Cogley the Mathematical Monkey calculates sums like a slide rule.

Given that approach, I'm even more eager to see what they sell in Custom's Instruments of Correction. Do they build the cages that go round the Carousel of Shame or do they make tubas that cure shortsightedness or stop you from using Oxford commas?

Of course, being a children's story, I'm sure it's nothing kinkier than that. Of course, being a children's story, there's a moral lesson to be imparted and, once that's done and dusted, all is forgiven and there's also a happy ending. It covers all the bases and does that well.

However, it also adds a sliver of sadness to that happy ending because Lt. Dimitrikov has been called to the front, but that's not hard to remedy in a sequel, which we clearly need to find out what happens next. Or, of course, we could just order the novels and keep our time with the Dellamorte sisters alive, which wasn't an option in 2018 but thankfully is now.

Before I wrap, I should mention that quite a few of the steampunk shorts covered in this book feature actors that you might know. This time, that's Gigi Edgely of *Farscape* fame, who voices Zarah Dellamorte.

DR. GRORDBORT PRESENTS: THE DEADLIEST GAME (2011)

DIRECTOR: JAMES CUNNINGHAM

WRITER: NICK WARD

STARS: GEOFF HOUTMAN, MORGANA O'REILLY AND SIMON MCKINNEY

Every time I watch *The Deadliest Game*, I find myself surprised all over again at how short it is. That's because it's so richly visualised that I remember it being much longer.

It's a film based on an existing property but not the usual sort of property, like a book. I've never been entirely sure what Dr. Grordbort is but I believe it began as a line of ray guns, Dr. Grordbort's Infallible Aether Oscillators, built as collectible models by Greg Broadmore, who works for Weta Workshop, the digital effects house created by Peter Jackson. In fact, he had finished working on Jackson's remake of *King Kong* when he conjured up these weapons and was about to start as the lead concept designer on *District 9*.

That since grew into art, books, boardgames and this short film, amongst whatever else has struck Broadmore as a good idea. I believe he still works for Weta but Dr. Grordbort remains a going concern.

His sprawling fictional universe is grounded in pulp fiction, from the ripping yarns of the Victorian era through the old boys papers to the sci-fi pulps of the thirties. However, it's all as satirical as it is nostalgic, which is why the outrageous machismo on offer in *The Deadliest Game* is glorious fun.

We don't meet Dr. Grordbort here, because he's merely responsible for making this short film possible and so lands a presenting credit. The lead character is Lord Broadforce, who is an amalgam of all the most British characters in Victorian fiction and he's portrayed to utter perfection by Geoff Houtman.

His negative side is completely obvious. He's a bloodthirsty soldier whose twenty thousand kills during the Venusian Wars may have been merely innocent villagers, as a journalist dares to point out. He's a big game hunter who picks weapons like golf clubs, caring nothing for the rarity of creatures except that they'll remain preserved forever within His Majesty's Society for the Study of Off-World Species's collection.

He's dismissive of anything a mere slip of a woman might have to say and, in a neat echo of the way in which neo-conservatives refuse to acknowledge personal pronouns they don't recognise, refuses to acknowledge the chosen title of Ms. Millicent Middlesworth, calling her Miss even after she corrects him. She happens to be that journalist,who's accompanying him on a factfinding mission and is horrified by his behaviour from moment one.

However, he's also the epitome of insanely brave, willing to put his life on the line to save the little lady, facing off against an incredibly large and horrible monster with nothing but his fists. He has the absolute confidence in his abilities and his God-given right to use them that comes with being British and of a certain period in history.

Really, he's not the hero of the story, even if he happens to be the hero of that moment, but Ms. Middlesworth, as progressive a character as he is traditional, isn't either. While she has every validity to question his motivations and his morals, it proves to be rather dangerous to question his experience.

If there's a hero here, it's Caruthers, who in the fine tradition of ripping yarns, serves Lord Broadforce as his butler. While his lordship is able to sit back, shoot things and act superior, Caruthers takes care of business. He drives the carriage, retrieves the heads of his employer's kills using a robotic elephant and, as we'll find, sacrifices himself for a good cause.

While there's really not a lot of story going on here, any conversation about it can't fail to find some serious depth because it taps deeply into the very essence of steampunk. Sure, it's absolutely gorgeous, this CGI imagining of the planet Venus joyously detailed, but the script pierces right to the heart of who we are. Yes, I mean you and me. Steampunks.

Now, every steampunk has an answer to the question, "What is steampunk?" and if we pool all our answers, maybe we'll start to approach the truth of it. It's certainly not just retro sci-fi in the vein of Jules Verne. It's just as certainly not just sticking a gear on it. The answer that rings truest to me is that it rewinds history so that we can do it right this time.

We thrill to the scientific adventures from Verne and Wells and, sure, the old boys papers that were such an influence on this film. We revel in the sheer invention of the Industrial Revolution and cheer the advances of science. We see beauty in handcrafted mahogany and brass. All of it speaks to us and we see little of

that today, so we're eager to rewind time and live back then when everyone was polite and worked for the betterment of mankind.

However, we're also very well aware that it wasn't like that. We're cherrypicking history and, while it was a glory era for some, it was hardly available to everyone. The class system prevented that, the oppression of women and the exploitation of children, on top of a habit of arriving in other people's countries and just claiming them as our own. The more we find out about the age that gave us such wonders, the more we learn about how far we've come in so many ways, and, quite naturally, we want the best of both worlds.

So we rewind time back to a certain point in the late nineteenth century and we promise to do it right this time. This film ably reminds us of both what we want to fix and what we want to keep, with how much there is of each ready for discussion on a convention panel. Politely, of course.

I mention all this because this plays to me as a steampunk short without hesitation, one of the truest such in this book. However, it's free otherwise of most of the usual details that we expect. I don't see any gears, for a start. These characters arrive on Venus in a spaceship and shoot rayguns. Their ambulatory carriage does not appear to run on steam. It fits thematically with the three human character archetypes of the steampunk age.

As mentioned already, Lord Broadforce is an establishment figure, colonialist nobility. Miss Middlesworth is the progressive, a woman in a profession whose questions are all good ones, even if she's out of her depth in the Venusian outback. And Caruthers is the servant, in more than one way, as we find.

So this is steampunk and it's brilliant.

ENTRE LES LIGNES (2015)

DIRECTORS: CHRISTELLE ALION, TOM CASACOLI, NOLWENN EVE, LORENN LE BEC AND EMMANUELLE REMY

WRITERS: CHRISTELLE ALION, TOM CASACOLI, NOLWENN EVE, LORENN LE BEC AND EMMANUELLE REMY

STARS: THIBAUD CHAUFOURIER AND CORALIE LESCOU

If we were stunned by how simple a sweet romance *The Craftsman* was, then this film, an even shorter and simpler sweet romance, will utterly blow us away. *Entre les Lignes* translates from the French to *Between the Lines* and it cuts everything away that it possibly can to leave just the lines and two people.

While the lines are also metaphorical, they appear here in physical form too as elevated monorail lines. We aren't told which city we're in, but it's a big one, judging from how many lines converge at a grand central station. The film is French and there's French writing on the carriages, so maybe this is Paris within an alternate steampunk universe or perhaps one of the larger provincial cities. Who knows? It's not important.

There's a story about to unfold on the lines in this city and it's exquisitely simple. A young man rides a train, presumably regularly. When it stops at a light in the station, it stops next to a train on a neighbouring rail and there, only a couple of feet away on the other side of two panes of glass and a short air gap, is a young woman reading a book. She's quite obviously the most beautiful creature he's ever seen and he falls immediately and totally in love.

After being stunned by that first moment, he relishes each further one, each day on their regular commutes, doing everything he can to conjure up a smile on her beautiful face. And she clearly appreciates him, until she starts to appear distracted and he starts to lose hope.

But, of course, there's a happy ending to be had, and it's not a difficult one to figure out. It feels right, even with the rise fall rise cadence to it, and it's aided by a beautiful and uplifting score by Aurélien Marini and Mark Scotto that warms the soul.

Just as the filmmakers cut the story down to its very essence, they did the same with their general approach. This isn't technically silent, given that we can hear the pistons of the train stopping and starting, but the two characters are in different trains, so they can't converse through regular dialogue and that means that there isn't any. So, even though it's not truly a silent film, it unfolds like one and that's fine.

After all, this particular story is written not only between the lines of this steam-powered monorail but on the faces of its characters too, and both actors were well cast for that to be at all possible.

The boy is Thibaud Chaufourier, who has a few credits on IMDb. The girl is Coralie Lescou, who doesn't. However, they're both perfect in this series of moments. He's characterful and quirky. She's elegant and sophisticated. They believably delight each other and that's what a romance is, really, between the lines.

And, just like *The Craftsman*, there's not a lot more I can say about this film, because you're not going to appreciate how truly right it feels until you watch it yourself.

I guess I could add that, bizarrely, given how pure and simple a romance it is, it was written and directed by no fewer than five people with writing direction (direction d'écriture) from a further three. Usually, writing by committee is a guarantee to bloat and complicate any script but this one avoids that blissfully.

I could also add that the credits, which run a minute and a half, so about a third of the story itself, are delightful, with little notes animated in French onto the credit cards and lines that represent the journeys of the characters there too, intertwining happily at the end.

And I could add that there doesn't seem to be a heck of a lot about this gem of a short film online, which is one reason why I curate and host these Roadshow sets and also why I write about short film at Apocalypse Later. This one was made and it was seen and it deserves a lot more credit than just a handful of comments on YouTube. Hopefully, writing about it here will help to ensure that it continues to reach new viewers, after which it'll live on in their hearts as well as mine.

Et oui, c'est ligne 42 pour les grand fans de *The Hitch-Hiker's Guide to the Galaxy*.

EUGEN: THE STEAMPUNK MUSICAL (2013)

DIRECTOR: DARIO RADUSIN

WRITER: DARIO RADUSIN

STARS: IGOR JAKLOVIĆ AND JELENA MARTINOVIĆ

Here's another romance, but told in a rather different way because it's also a musical.

I often wonder why this hasn't been done a lot more often, because I know a whole slew of steampunks who would seem more than able to do the idea justice, but my musical friends seem to prefer to make music videos rather than musicals. It took a production company from Croatia to do it justice.

I should add that it's entirely musical. There are no lines of dialogue here, as everything is told through song. And that's a good thing for me because my neurodivergent brain always bristles at musicals. The ones I like either have story reasons for people breaking into song at the drop of a hat, like, say, *Singin' in the Rain*, or are told entirely through song so that we only have to suspend disbelief once and we're done, like in, say, *The Umbrellas of Cherbourg*.

So this works for me. So do the songs, which are universally perky, even when the villain of the piece is outlining her dastardly plan. None of them are soporific, even the happy reunion song at the end that sets up the happy ending. I can't sing along much because I don't know a lot of Croatian, but I can attempt it from how it sounds and I find myself doing it every time I watch. "Dobar dan, dobar dan..."

I found *Eugen* relatively early on in my quest for steampunk films to screen at conventions, but I didn't screen it until recently because it's only online in its native Croatian without any English subtitles to help people like me out.

I did think about seeking permission from the filmmakers anyway, as the story is easy to figure out from the action alone, as both Igor Jaklović and Jelena Martinović, the two leads, are highly expressive actors. However, in the end, I realised that I could simply ask if they already had English subtitles, which they did. I did tweak them a little to be smoother but that wasn't hard to do, given the context.

That story is relatively straightforward and neatly universal, but I'm guessing there's also a little more oomph to the relationship for an audience who understands the nuances of the Croatian culture. Would depth in that cultural background help? I think so. Is it needed? Not at all. Would Professor Eugen benefit from an American cultural background to better grok the Cherie Priest novels he has on the shelf in his office, like *Boneshaker* and *Dreadnought*? I'd say so. Does he need that? Not at all. I adored them and this and I'm English.

The professor works in Zagreb, the capital of Croatia, at the Faculty of Engineering, and he apparently doesn't like it much. That's less of a reflection on Croatia or his university and more about his time. The word floated at the very outset is "hectic". He's had enough of it. He wants to travel back to a simpler time and plans to do exactly that using a time machine. As we join him, today is the day. He's ready to go back to 1892 and he's joyful at the thought.

Now, Eugen looks retro to begin with. Even in his office, he sports a bow tie and waistcoat and they suit him. Sure, he goes home first to change into outright steampunk garb before making his jaunt through time, but he doesn't need to. He's effortlessly retro.

Sandra, however, is far more deliberate in a retro look. She looks appropriately enticing in her black and red villain's outfit but she's very much dressing to impress rather than for any thought towards comfort, even though she's a working engineer, putting the final touches to her dastardly plan in Eugen's laboratory.

You see, she doesn't want him to go back in time. She clearly loves him but he's taken her for granted and plans to leave her behind. He does tell her that he loves her before switches are thrown, that he'll miss her and even that she could come with him so they could make a better life for themselves in 1892, but she has to go through with her plan to ensure that he truly notices her.

The happy ending is that she succeeds, as I'd guess you've already figured out, because she isn't so much of a villain as she plays, with her elegantly maniacal laugh. She's a woman who wants to be seen by the man she loves and has found no other way to achieve that. And now, time is running out and she even has to send him on his way. What would you do?

I'm not entirely sure about the logistics of what follows but I'm not going to argue with a steampunk musical about what's realistic. The message stands and it's a good one, even if I'm not aware of anyone quite so dedicated to the Victorian era as Professor Eugen has become, even within the steampunk scene.

And, of course, I'll happily accept that there was no better way for Sandra to get her point across to the oblivious Professor, entirely for the sake of the story. I'm utterly oblivious to flirting myself but I can't imagine not noticing any character played by Jelena Martinović and especially one who wears outfits like this one and endows her songs with such raw emotion.

I can also see why she fell for the Professor too, though what I found myself admiring the most about him isn't something I expected to ever admire in anyone. It's the elastic way that Igor Jaklović moves, because he has a knack of throwing his head back then walking forward that I've only ever seen done before in cartoon characters. I get what he's doing and why and it's a great way to show how confident he is in his skin and also how carefree he is, but it's not remotely as easy as it looks. I'd walk into walls if I tried that! How can anyone move forward while they're looking at the ceiling, especially in a sort of dance move because he's also singing a song at the same time. That's impressive and he makes it seem effortless.

So, while I'd heartily recommend that more steampunks should make steampunk musicals —and, please, folk, explain to me why nobody else has—this is a worthy first entry into that niche subgenre. If you seek this out, as I hope you will, be aware that the version that writer and director Dario Radusin posted to YouTube is in Croatian without English subtitles, but I also hope that this review is all that you need to help you through it.

Or just sing along in Croatian... "Dobar dan, dobar dan, tako svaki dan!" All together now!

A GENTLEMEN'S DUEL (2006)

DIRECTORS: FRANCISCO RUIZ AND SEAN MCNALLY

WRITERS: SEAN MCNALLY, FRANCISCO RUIZ, JEFF FOWLER AND TIM MILLER

STARS: TOM KENNY, ASHLEY WALSH AND CHUCK WOJTKIEWICZ

A Gentlemen's Duel isn't quite the oldest film in this zine, nudged away from that honour by a pair of 2005 films, *The Mysterious Geographic Explorations of Jasper Morello* and *The Unusual Inventions of Henry Cavendish*, but it was the first film that I ever screened at a steampunk convention, way back in 2014 when Wild Wild West Steampunk Convention III was held at Old Tucson Studios and we used the screen in the saloon. That was quite the experience!

I've watched it many times since then and I brought it to San Diego in 2019 when I realised that I hadn't screened at Gaslight Steampunk Expo yet. It's just as much fun on every return visit, but I've only just discovered that one of the voice actors is Tom Kenny, the voice since the very beginning of SpongeBob SquarePants. It seems that he was aware of steampunk long before I was, because I only stumbled upon it in 2010, courtesy of Steampunk Street in Mesa.

Kenny voices the quintessential Englishman here, who may or may not be burdened by the rather unfortunate name of Sir Dingleberry. It seems entirely appropriate, but may just be an insult from his quintessentially French enemy, who may or may not be similarly dubbed the Marquis de Moundstrumpet, possibly also an entirely appropriate insult, just like Monsieur Poopypants. Who knows?

Regardless of what their true names are, the situation at hand is that they are both wooing the Lady, who has no name but is voiced with sounds but never words by Ashley Young. She may be non-verbal, even if it's just because the pair of bickering suitors don't give her even an opportunity to get a word in, but she has quite the impressive cleavage, only surpassed in size and elegance by her country estate, so it's not difficult to see the attraction.

As you might imagine from the title, their ceaseless verbal jabs and constant attempts to outdo each other's efforts to impress the Lady quickly escalates into an outright duel but one between supposed gentlemen.

What that means to us is that they suit up in an incomprehensibly resilient steam-powered pair of mecha suits that they've conveniently stashed in the trees a short distance away. And then they go at it with wild abandon.

This is all animated in stylish 3D animation, the sort of thing that we might expect from a studio like Pixar. Blur Studio may not be quite so well known but they've been around since 1995 working on a range of media, including games, feature films and commercials. They've recently stepped up their original content by producing *Love, Death & Robots* for Netflix. That was created by the founder of Blur Studio, Tim Miller, who served as co-writer and executive producer here. He had been nominated for an Oscar already with an animated short called *Gopher Broke*, but he then went on to make his feature directorial debut with no lesser a film than the first *Deadpool* movie.

While this is 3D animation, it adheres to the rules of 2D cartoon violence, meaning that the unnamed Lady is bashed, bruised and battered constantly in the periphery of the fighting but never looks any worse for wear. Of course, it helps that she has a very capable butler who is almost always in the right place to shield her from the worst of it. As you might imagine, he is the real hero of the day, rather than the pair of careless, clumsy nemeses who wreak havoc and destruction wherever they happen to go.

It's this firm adherence to cartoon rules that makes this work so well, because we never feel that anyone's in danger. I'm sure there are lots of people we'd like to pound into oblivion, but only if it wouldn't actually hurt them. And, at the end of the day, they're still gentlemen. We know that because they stop for tea when the butler rings his little bell. Then they resume as they left off, because honour is at stake here!

Another success is the detailing, which had to have taken plenty of time to render back in 2006 when computers weren't as powerful as they are now. These two mecha are gorgeous creations, the Englishman's being intricately detailed on the outside while the Frenchman's is luxuriously upholstered inside. There's even a throne in there for his armoured poodle, Fifi.

Of course, the Frenchman's suit simply had to resemble a frog, because stereotypical slurs are fair game between these combatants, but I can't see an equivalent stereotypical slur on the Englishman's mecha. It looks rather like a mole to me but I wasn't aware that the French used that as a pejorative for their traditional enemies on the other side of the Channel.

More obviously pejorative are the weapons that they bring to bear, because each of them has a secret weapon to fall back on when they need it most.

The Englishman's is what I have to describe as fishpunk, even though Rick Novy, a local author here in Arizona, didn't create that until 2012 with a novel of that name. What it means here is that the Englishman is able to harness the power of electric eels, naturally secreted within brass tanks in his mecha, to deliver an electric shock to his opponent, down his more traditional extensible chain whip.

In response, the Frenchman's is what could only be called a crotch rocket, a telescopic gun situated exactly where you think it is, which he uses to fire a ravenous Fifi at his enemy.

As you might imagine from all I've said thus far, the sense of humour here is a little ribald, but there's nothing entirely untoward that's shown on screen. In other words, this is quite appropriate for children, but they may not see exactly the same jokes that adults can't fail to notice. But hey, doesn't that go for *SpongeBob SquarePants* too?

Now, how do I acquire one of these mecha suits? I promise not to use it to crush a rival in order to get closer to a pair of boobies. Much.

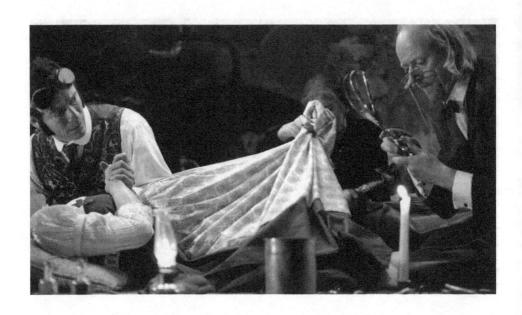

THE GIRL WITH THE MECHANICAL MAIDEN (2013)

DIRECTOR: ANDREW LEGGE

WRITER: ANDREW LEGGE

STARS: DOMINIC WEST, SERENA BRABAZON, INGRID CRAIGIE AND SOPHIE SCULLY

To the best of my knowledge, only a single filmmaker is represented by two films in this zine and that's writer/director Andrew Legge, who had made *The Unusual Inventions of Henry Cavendish* in 2005 and returned to this sort of period setting eight years later for *The Girl with the Mechanical Maiden*.

It's a lavish production, shot at Birr Castle in the Irish midlands, the home of the 7th Earl of Rosse, which was built in the 17th century. It's appropriate to set a science fiction story there because it has a real science history. It's home to the Leviathan of Parsonstown, which was the largest reflecting telescope in the world for over seventy years, from 1845 to 1917, and the oldest darkroom in existence, that of Mary Parsons, wife of the 3rd Earl of Rosse, who was a pioneering 19th century photographer.

Small wonder that it's home here to a man who's surrounded himself with robots that he built out of whatever he had to hand. They're all humanoid but they rarely look human, the accoutrements they wear instead of hands not the only obvious discrepancies. Each is clearly designed for a specific function, whether that be to cut wood or clean. I particularly like the one whose head looks like a hairdryer. That's presumably what it exists for.

There are only two other human beings in the place—his wife and the housekeeper—but that doesn't change as the former gives birth to a daughter because it's her final act. She's

shocked by a charge from some sort of huge steam device and falls to the ground. While an obstetrician saves the baby, he can't save her.

That throws the inventor into a whole new world for which he's physically not equipped, but he does what he does. Learning about wet nurses from an old book on infant husbandry, he doesn't hire one, he builds one. She looks a lot like Maria from *Metropolis* and she lactates, in some fashion that's oddly sustainable.

Unfortunately, the housekeeper, in the long tradition of old Irish women believing things to be against the will of the Almighty, storms in to rescue the baby from the creature. Sadly, her ill-advised plans backfire, quite literally, as the scuffle that ensues damages another steam device and a huge explosion takes care of both the inventor and the housekeeper.

Only the baby survives, buried by rubble but kept safe by the wet nurse robot, who has now become much more than that. With the estate locked up by the townsfolk and left alone, she has also become the child's mother and father.

Now, that may well sound like I've provided a synopsis of the entire film but that's only the first five minutes to set up the real story. What follows is all about the girl, who like everyone else is not named, and the mechanical maiden who raises her. It's a touching story, one that always reminds me of the scenes between the monster and the girl in *Frankenstein*, but with a better programmed monster.

There's much to praise here, but the people involved were hardly new. Legge had already won multiple awards for two period pieces of interest to steampunks, *The Unusual Inventions of Henry Cavendish*, covered within these pages; and *The Chronoscope*, a faux documentary from 2010 about a 1930s Irish woman who invents a machine that can look into the past but is then forgotten by history. He's also won awards for *Lola*, a feature released in 2022, which switches that around, its machine intercepting TV and radio broadcasts from the future.

The inventor is played by Dominic West, an English actor of Irish heritage best known for his Golden Globe-winning performance in *The Wire*. His film roles are as varied as *Spice World*, *Chicago* and *John Carter*. He's currently playing King Charles III, as the Prince of Wales, in the TV show *The Crown*.

You might recognise the obstetrician as Ned Dennehy from such TV shows as *Peaky Blinders*, *Good Omens* and *Outlander*. Ingrid Craigie, who plays the housekeeper, seems acutely familiar to me too, though I can't tell where I know her from. The point is that everyone involved has serious credentials and absolutely lives up to their roles, even though nobody gets to speak.

Like *Entre les Lignes*, this is not a silent film, because we hear everything we ought to hear, from robots clanking through the hallways to the cries of a newborn baby, and including, of course, the explosion that kills the inventor. It just doesn't have any dialogue. The actors are all tasked with doing their jobs without words.

Regardless of the credentials of those actors I've already mentioned, the one who does best at this is Serena Brabazon, not so much as the inventor's wife, because she has precious little screen time in that role, but in her other part as the mechanical maiden. We don't see her at all, because she's encased in metal, but we do see her move and she's delightfully expressive as she works ceaselessly to take care of a child she was only ever supposed to nurse.

Brabazon is a trained professional actor and she has a string of credits to her name, but it can't be said that she's prolific because most of her roles are in films directed by her husband, including this one. I'm guessing that it was her connections that landed this pristine shooting location too, as she's also Lady Brabazon, the daughter of the 15th Earl of Meath. Certainly the extras listed as members of the inevitable mob—I did mention *Frankenstein*—include such notables as Lord Meath and the Hon. Michael Parsons, the latter of whom didn't have much of a commute given that he lives at Birr Castle.

This connection to history gives me wonder why there aren't more steampunk films made in the British Isles. I grew up there and I know that everywhere I went, history was visible all around me. There are entire towns that would serve as sets for steampunk films without the need for much dressing up. It's just one reason why British television is rightly known for its period dramas. However, the thirty films I've included in this zine only include two made in the UK, one of them animated, and a couple in Ireland, both of the latter courtesy of one filmmaker, Andrew Legge.

It's not like there aren't steampunks all over the old country. There are. I've stumbled into them in charity shops. However, it seems that, for some unknown reason, they simply don't happen to be filmmakers. I wonder why.

In the meantime, I guess we have to imagine how many steampunk films could have been produced in locations as genuine as this and with actors of this quality and experience.

INVENTION OF LOVE (2010)

DIRECTOR: ANDREY SHUSHKOV
WRITER: ANDREY SHUSHKOV

Invention of Love is another romance, a "love story from the world of gears and bolts", but it doesn't end happily like *The Craftsman* or *Entre les Lignes*. This is a sad romance, from fatalistic Russia, and it's a warning against the ongoing mechanisation of society, made while Andrey Shushkov was studying at the Saint Petersburg State University of Culture and Arts. This is his final presentation piece.

Like both *Entre les Lignes* and *The Girl with the Mechanical Maiden*, it's a silent film with sound effects but no dialogue. However, while those films were live action, this is animated and in a very particular style, that of the silhouette.

Now, there's serious precedent here because the oldest surviving animated feature film was made using the very same silhouette style. It's *The Adventures of Prince Achmed*, made by Lotte Reiniger in Germany and released in 1926. It's a wonderful feature, based on stories from the *Arabian Nights*, and it's easy to find today.

It also has a pedigree in steampunk cinema. *The Mysterious Geographic Explorations of Jasper Morello*, the oldest film in this zine, unfolds in silhouette, albeit in 3D rather than entirely 2D, and there are silhouette scenes as far back as *Invention for Destruction* in 1958, released in the U.S. as *The Fabulous World of Jules Verne*.

Here, the silhouettes are all 2D, with any 3D effects provided through layering, even in the early scenes that feature passing clouds. I'ts all beautiful work and, after panning through the wreckage of the man's house, we feel his pain as he dives into his memories to remember his true love while she was alive.

She's a country girl and he meets her while out riding his mechanical horse. We listen to piano and violin while they frolic in the fields under a beautiful full moon. And time passes. They kiss. They marry. He takes her home in a flying ship hoisted by balloons and propelled by steam power.

But he lives in the city and she quickly finds that it isn't just his horse and his ship that are machines. Everything's mechanised in the city from the cars and the carriages all the way to the trees and the butterflies. The flower shop sells moving plants made of metal and even a pig in a top hat turns out to be clockwork.

The only thing in the city that's natural is a plant that she keeps on her window sill, but it dies and her husband throws it away, building her a mechanical equivalent instead. She runs down a long spiral staircase to find it amongst the rubble under the city, but it's a dead thing now and the pollutants make her cough.

She sickens and she dies and, of course, her widower builds a replacement out of metal he salvages from whatever machines he can find in his house. And here, at last, he realises what he's truly lost because his dead wife is the only natural thing he knew and a metal version can never replace her.

I've told the entire film here, which I prefer not to do because I hate spoilers, but then the opening scene set us up for this, so it's hardly a surprise. Also, the whole point of the film is the message at the end, so it's impossible to do *Invention of Love* justice without taking you all the way to it.

If I'd set you up by pointing out that the two of them meet and fall in love and marry, you'd think that this was a sweet romance like *Entre les Lignes* and it isn't, even when it kinda sorta is. This man, whoever he is, finds a wonder but never truly understands why until she's gone and he learns that he can't simply replace her.

Then again, maybe I could have just pointed out that this was Russian, with the implication that it was going to end with death. There's an entirely accurate meme doing the rounds that looks at literature from different countries. In England, a character will die for honour, in the U.S. for freedom and in France for love. In the literature of Russia, that character will simply die, with no reason needed.

What that would have missed is the emotion inherent in this short film. Because Shushkov didn't give us names or details—we never find out who these people are or where they live— it ought to be impersonal, but the score, which unfolds in piano and violin, some original and some taken from Chopin, takes our hearts on a real journey and we soar and plummet with an unnamed silhouette character who never says a word. That's filmmaking skill.

It's also a strong reminder of a lesson that I learned in the art of programming short films, one I've benefitted from in subsequent sets in the Roadshow and at my full film festival. The films I select have to be worthy, of course, but the order in which they're presented can be as important. There's a need to flow, for films to connect to each other, and it's important to be aware of the emotional arc that they carry.

I learned the latter lesson at Wild Wild West Steampunk Convention III, because I included this film in a set whose emotional arc started at a neat high with *A Gentleman's Duel* but then fell and fell and it was too much. Fortunately, I brought it back up at the end with comedy and music, but I'd let people drop too long.

While I've programmed this much better at later events, it benefits from isolation. It's the sort of film that's well worth watching—and it is viewable on YouTube—but then sitting back and thinking about, rather than going straight into another movie. There's meaning here and it needs time to resonate.

So check it out. I heartily recommend it. Let the music wash over you as you enjoy the neat silhouette animation, let your heart swell with the blue tinting in the happy scenes and break when the vibrant young lady dies and the man she leaves behind learns his lesson. But then take time to think about it, to wonder how far you've let your life be mechanised and all the natural wonders that you might be missing.

It's a perfect example of how steampunk is able to take us back in time and yet speak to us about today.

And don't worry! There's plenty to perk you back up later in the book!

THE LAST EAGLE (2018)

DIRECTOR: JEAN-CHRISTOPHE DRUEZ

WRITER: JEAN-CHRISTOPHE DRUEZ

STARS: MAËVA DRUEZ, J. C. DRUEZ, YANN JOLY, HAROLD HOUISSE AND RAPHAEL PARELLADA

The Last Eagle is something of an anomaly in this zine for a couple of reasons, but I feel that it's still worthy of inclusion here because it's a highly unusual and immersive film with some wonderful steampunk visuals.

One is that it's not really a short film but it's not a feature either, running what my festival programming brain tells me is a very awkward forty-two minutes. That's half of a feature.

The other is that the story makes it feel like half a feature too, because, while we certainly get from A to B, B doesn't solve the problems set in A and it sets a whole lot more in motion which aren't addressed because it finishes just a little later. So we need the second half of the feature to tell us how all these plot strands are wrapped up. I don't know if Jean-Christophe Druez even plans to do that.

However, what he did do is fascinating, both in its set-up and its realisation which, through a quirk of circumstance, sits relatively unique among its peers.

The set-up is a richly imagined steampunk universe, in which a Transatlantic Empire has been forged by the time we start in 1879. The technology is steam-powered, of course, so the need for a source of energy over such a scale is huge and the demands on the planet great.

Professor Cornwell discovers the solution in a substance called Aerolium. The crystals that are synthesised to hold it can be recharged by electricity and airships stuck mid-flight can do that by harnessing bolts of lightning. It's great stuff and it promises much for this empire.

Of course, there's a catch and that arrives a dozen years later in Mayfield, Utah when one Aerolium production facility blows up. The gas released in the explosion is toxic and its sweep across the land kills everything in its path. The solution has become the problem and nothing seems to help.

That's a little unusual already, but instead of figuring out a solution to the new problem, as he did the old, Cornwell decides to go back in time so that he can change everything before it all goes horribly wrong. After all, he has an impressively ornate time machine; of course he should put it to good use. After consulting a tarot deck, which is an interesting touch, he leaves a note for his daughter and vanishes.

And we're only four minutes into forty-two. There's a lot to come, but I should explain the way that Druez put this together.

This is live action, but much of the backdrop is clearly CGI. It looks really good, detailed and inventive, but it doesn't look like live action. It looks like real actors performing in front of a green screen and placed into CGI backgrounds, the result being rather like a videogame. On a first glimpse, it's a little disconcerting because we can see that it's not all real, but the film's length helps because we get used to it quickly and start seeing it as the neat aesthetic choice that it never truly was.

So, while we don't buy into this CGI as being real towns and ships and gadgets, we revel in how inventive and impeccably detailed it is.

For instance, we spend most of our time on an airship called the *Last Eagle* and it's a beast of a ship, a carefully designed marvel that any steampunk worth his or her salt is guaranteed to ache to travel on. It's lavishly furnished all the way down to the individual gadgets, which appropriately for a Transatlantic Empire, are labelled in different languages, depending on where they were made. The supplies also have labels showing that they came from multiple countries. The detail goes as far as every clock being ornately designed and the ship's log is a thing of true beauty indeed.

It's called an Aronautica and I would dearly love to play with it. It records audio onto a roll rather like a wax cylinder but with impressive storage capability. A rotary mechanism allows navigation through the recording down to the very second. A gramophone horn provides the playback medium. It's all incorporated into an octagonal table and everything's made out of wood and brass. It's quintessential steampunk gadgetry and it works like a charm to provide a key discovery in the story.

You see, Cornwell's daughter is on the *Last Eagle*, but she's on her own. Captain Barlow is a traitor who betrayed the professor and took off with his crew, but he's not so evil that he'd throw a teenage girl overboard, so he has her drugged and she wakes up with a chance to do what must be done to survive.

As Mlle. Cornwell is played by Maëva Druez, I presume she's the director's daughter, and I would have assumed that even had I not seen her name in the credits. It's obvious that she's not a professional actor but she brings charm and pluck to the role, especially after deciding to figure out the ship's location with sextant, astronomical tables and charts, and switches to manual control to fly it herself.

And she ably carries this film for well over ten minutes until she bumps into a mysterious stowaway who appears out of nowhere while she's struggling to regain control of the ship after a pressure alert prompts engine failure. Even then, they're the only two characters for the next seventeen minutes and this stranger is confined behind a leather gas mask so every moment of emotion has to come from Maëva.

When we do meet someone else, excluding the Professor in brief flashback scenes, it's the Professor somewhere else entirely, which I'm not going to spoil and you're unlikely to guess because there's nothing to prepare us for it.

While I have to say it was a little jarring on my first viewing, I'm a big fan of where Druez went with his story, because there's so much depth and possibility to where it can continue. The caveat is, of course, that it needs to and I don't know that it will. This was released onto Vimeo as a short film, rather than as the first in a series of webseries episodes.

And here's the danger for indie filmmakers who work in such a niche genre as steampunk. Many have the ambition to create something substantial and few have the wherewithall to make it happen. *1873: The Insidious Intrigue* and *The Mechanical Grave* are beginnings and, in a perfect world, they'd be continued in further instalments, but, in both instances, reality had the filmmakers go onto other projects. This is a huge achievement for a very small team and a massively ambitious one. That they nailed it here gives me hope that there will be a second half to this story, or indeed multiple further episodes. Only time will tell!

MASK OF VENGEANCE (2016)

DIRECTOR: CORY MCBURNETT

WRITER: PHILLIP STEIN

STARS: JOHN STRANGEWAY, JOE HARRIS, DAVID LEE, CHRIS ROSENOW, TONY BALLARD-SMOOT, PHILLIP STEIN, CLIFFTON TURNELL, PAIGE GARDNER AND DEVAN HENDERSON

One of the first steampunk celebrities that I ever met was Steampunk Boba Fett, and John Strangeway, the man behind the character, is still one of the most engaging. As stoic as he is as this character, he's a pixie out of the helmet and he has a habit of gatecrashing the better half's fashion shows. Him chasing Alex Canto's Steampunk BB-8 around the stage impromptu is a favourite memory of mine.

Because Boba Fett is a cinematic character, it was inevitable that his steampunk version would make it into films too and that began in 2013 with a short called *Trial of the Mask*. It's a decent film and I was happy to screen it in one of my Roadshow sets, but its only sequel thus far, *Mask of Vengeance*, is far superior.

That first film does what it needs to. Fett is hired by Steampunk Darth Vader, in the form of steampunk artist, author and large vehicle builder, David Lee, wearing his own costume, to locate and kill a jedi called Kala'myr, which he promptly does. However, there's a catch to the story that we learn late that complicates it just a little. There's some decent CGI and some good scenes and it's worth watching, however cheesy the asteroid cloud montage is.

However, the second film does more than it needs to. It's much more ambitious right from the start, with much better CGI, a holographic battle room display and even a brief battle in space. David Lee returns as Steampunk Darth

Vader and there's Steampunk R2D2 as well. It feels snappier and it gets neatly onto business. Sure, there's a landspeeder with a gear on it to call it steampunk, but the rest of the design is excellent and I ain't complainin'.

The music's better, the travel scene is busier and there's a very cool character calling Fett to seek an audience with Jabba. I recognise the design, so that's Paige Gardner as Eera Pax. It all feels richer and more immersive, with the far more sprawling cast soon evident, with an abundance of extras to flesh out the backdrop.

Joe Harris is an evocative Steampunk Jabba the Hutt and his throne room has a wealth of Twi'leks, including one highly expressive bald slave girl. He has a neat floating robot to man the door and, keeping with *Star Wars* tradition, there's plenty of multilingual dialogue. Phillip Stein also wrote some neatly succinct humour into that dialogue too. Fett never uses a dozen words where one would do and Jabba praises him with, "You're my kind of scum!"

The Hutt wants Fett to find Crest Dayfall, a former associate who robbed him blind, and to bring him back alive. Of course he does so, but there are other stories to be told on the way, featuring new characters and ones tied to *Trial of the Mask*. This is a direct sequel, after all, and it picks up right as that film leaves off.

In fact, it ends up being rather surprising to find that the credits arrive just eleven minutes in. It's not that the film feels long; it just does a lot more than we expect it to be able to cram into such a short running time.

No wonder that it's racked up five thousand views on YouTube when so many other short steampunk films languish in the hundreds or even the tens of views. I'm actually surprised that it's that low, given how Mandalorians are such a big deal in the *Star Wars* universe now. Everything Strangeway did predates their rise in *The Mandalorian*.

And that's a shame, though it's also highly understandable. When people saw steampunk as a fad, here today and gone tomorrow, there was a lot of sense to taking existing characters from pop culture and designing equivalents in a steampunk universe as an intellectual and a crafting exercise. This one, appearing in a pair of films, certainly travelled more mileage than most, but it's far from alone.

However, as we know, steampunk was never a fad for the devotees. I'm still presenting film sets at Wild Wild West Con a decade on from starting out with *A Gentlemen's Duel* in 2013 and the better half is still organising their fashion show. However, our steampunk personae have evolved considerably since then. Henry, Count Chaos is a very different character now than he was when I MC'd my first fashion show.

Of course, I have all the flexibility I need to do that because I made him up. Steampunks like John Strangeway who adapted characters from pop culture didn't have that luxury. The character was the character. They could shift their design over time but they were stuck as a relatively static character and that gets old for the person in the costume as much as anyone else appreciating it from afar.

It bristles a little that someone might make an excellent Steampunk Mandalorian costume today and be rightly praised for it, but by folk who don't realise that Strangeway blazed that path long ago, in a galaxy far, far away. Such is the cost of being a pioneer, I guess.

Fortunately, there's evidence, not only in a slew of convention photos but in these two fan films. I've seen a lot of fan films in my day and they've grown in stature over time to include professionals working for fun. Check out a *Star Wars* fan film titled *Han Solo: A Smuggler's Trade*, which stars no less a talent than Doug Jones of *Hocus Pocus*, *Hellboy* and *Pan's Labyrinth* fame. I could also throw out Peter Jackson's *King Kong* as an example of a $207m fan film, but that is a little bit of a stretch, even if I'll back it up.

What surprised me here is that my last time through *Mask of Vengeance* would have been in the before times, pre-COVID, and yet it stands up very well to a fresh viewing. While *Trial of the Mask* feels like a fan film, *Mask of Vengeance* doesn't, except through some amateur acting from minor characters.

In particular, the CGI holds up, even though that's the element that tends to date quickest. I've always liked how it played into the design of Strangeway's existing costume. The sound design is good, with strong effects and foreign tongues. There's even a song here, *D.E.V.I.L.* by a southern gothic swing band from Carrollton, Georgia called Mayhayley's Grave, which is a catchy tune that somehow fits perfectly. The guest stars are all wonderful and the writing wraps them all up into a clever story.

Surprisingly, there aren't more fan films in the steampunk world. This is the only true one in this zine, for instance, though I can see an argument for *Nemo* being a Jules Verne fan film, even though it isn't. It's more common in music videos and Steampunk Boba Fett turns up in one of those too, *Steampunk Style*.

THE MECHANICAL GRAVE (2012)

DIRECTOR: JON KEEYES

WRITER: CHARLES BURNLEY, BASED ON A STORY BY CHARLES BURNLEY AND JON KEEYES

STARS: JONATHAN BROOKS, NICOLE LEIGH, MATTHEW TOMPKINS, MICHAEL CRABTREE AND CHARLES BAKER

Another subgenre of steampunk shockingly neglected by steampunk film is urban fantasy. Most steampunk films adopt sci-fi or alternate history as their genre, but there's just as much potential in horror and urban fantasy, as this wonderful short demonstrates. It's wide open for a sequel or second episode and could easily be turned into a TV show to sit alongside such efforts as *Penny Dreadful* and *Carnival Row*.

The Mechanical Grave plays very much in the ballpark of the former, or indeed *The League of Extraordinary Gentlemen*, mixing imaginary new characters with others we know from history, merely steampunked up a little.

The first of those is Edgar Allan Poe, who is less than fifty years dead in 1895, when this is set. His soul is now housed in an automaton and serves as one of two leaders of the Office of Esoteric Sciences. Jonathan Brooks, prolific as a voice actor, does a wonderfully unphased job as Poe here, curious and insightful but not shaken by anything, not unlike a steampunk take on Data in *Star Trek: The Next Generation*, in the physical form of Poe, of course.

While we glimpse him first and all the early dialogue is about him, we meet another name from history first, that being Teddy Roosevelt, not yet the 26th president of the United States but in this steampunk universe Commissioner of Police in whichever town we're in. This was shot in Dallas, but I'm thinking it's meant to be New York, given that his best local cop is Det. Wayne. It doesn't matter. It could be any city, though we are definitely in America.

We're also in an America in which science is on the ascendant, with steam-powered ships, clockwork robots and electricity beginning to take over. However, magic also exists, perhaps struggling to survive in a technological world but still very much present. The introductory text hints of Hereditary Magicians.

It may be that Poe's colleague, with whom he leads the Office of Esoteric Sciences, set up to protect America from supernatural threats, is an assassin, Mrs. Emma Louise Entwistle, a gothic steampunk version of Kate Beckinsale's characters in a variety of films, but surely also an homage to Emma Peel of *The Avengers* and also Mina Harker in *The League of Extraordinary Gentlemen.*

Matthew Tompkins plays Roosevelt, Nicole Leigh Mrs. Entwistle, and, with Brooks as Poe, they're three members of the team that would tackle the ambitious villains behind the world domination plot that would run through a set of further short films. Unfortunately, this sits alone because none of those have been made, but I have to wonder who else would belong to this team, whether fictional or historical.

The only villains we meet this time out are lackeys who attack during the finalé, some of them recognisable in steampunk groups such as Airship Isabella. Others I haven't met yet hail from the Celestial Rogues, the Mal do Ojo and the Steampunk Illumination Society. They all came in their own elaborate costumes with their own weapons and props, further devices being provided by Airship Nocturne and S. S. Kali's Hourglass.

There's another bad guy too, but he's not so much allied with the villains as present due to their ineptitude. The crime that everyone's in the film to investigate is a mass murder, which Poe soon ascertains was a ritual sacrifice, high magic used to conjure up an entity from Hell. Yes, a demon, and it manifests in the glorious form of Charles Baker, who plays Neshrew like Russell Brand playing Jack Sparrow.

That should be enough to get you going and eager to seek out this short, but I ought to add that it is neatly horrific. We spend our entire time in the foyer and front room of a mansion, which is also a crime scene, so corpses are not lacking. One of my favourite moments arrives when Neshrew magically wakes up a corpse as if it's a puppet, only for her to notice in horror that she's been sacrificed and so screams her lungs out, at which point he gestures her right back down into quiet death once more.

I have other favourite moments too, one of them not arriving until the end credits when I realised that two of the police officers utterly out of place around magic are honestly named Abercrombie and Fitch.

It's fair to say that those moments are well divvied up between Entwistle, who has quite a habit of dramatic entrances and exits; Poe, an accomplished deliverer of understated speech; and Roosevelt, who has plenty of secrets in his pocket, perhaps quite literally. All that goes as much for the finalé, in which they each get an opportunity to shine, as the bulk of the film, a

much quieter affair. Baker, of course, steals an entire section of the film, which is appropriate for a "vain little bugger" like him, to borrow a phrase from Commissioner Roosevelt.

The weak side of the film is surely its end, in part because the villainous lackeys who attack during the finalé are just cannon fodder to set up the talents of the leads, but mostly because that's the last thing we see. In a series, that's a highly fitting way to start, because the villains will no doubt get more and more dangerous as the episodes run on until we finally meet the big bad evil genius behind the entire plot, who I would love to identify if I only knew. But the series didn't happen and so we're left with this bunch of well dressed minions being the sum total of the dark side in this universe. That's a shame but, as it's been over a decade since *The Mechanical Grave* was released, it would seem likely that any continuation would warrant an entire recasting for a reboot, whether as a new series or as a feature film.

Alternatively, of course, the story could be continued in a different medium, whether in a series of comic books or novels. Subgenres like steampunk horror and urban fantasy are very much established in both. Highland Myst, the production company here, says on its website that the writer Charles Burnley's life has been steeped in literature and he's written at least four features. How about a novel, sir?

MONSTRUS CIRCUS (2019)

DIRECTOR: JORDAN INCONSTANT
WRITER: JORDAN INCONSTANT
STARS: JORIS ADU, JORDAN INCONSTANT, LOUIS DONVAL AND BERNARD FARCY

I first encountered French filmmaker Jordan Inconstant when he submitted a short film to ALIFFF, my film festival, in its first year. That was *Yo Soy Pedro*, a ten minute science fiction comedy about an alien arriving in Hollywood and everyone mistaking him for an actor in an alien suit. It's a fun and fast-paced ride and I'm very happy to have selected it, but this is a far more ambitious production in every way.

It's a long short, for a start, running half an hour. It has an ensemble cast, with quite a few cast members returning from *Yo Soy Pedro* for more substantial roles. It has an international scope, shifting from France to Scotland a third of the way in, with an additional scene shot in Switzerland at the Musée HR Giger. However, given that every character in Scotland speaks French, I'd guess that they may only be there through the magic of cinema.

And it has a serious message, one that's not just sprung on us at the end, like the reason it was primarily set in Scotland; it's inextricably woven throughout the entire film.

That message is tolerance, designed around the fact that most of the lead characters aren't like the rest of us. They all look very different, for one reason or another, and there's an easy word to describe them but Inconstant himself, playing Auguste the clown, cleverly sets us in motion at the very beginning, asking us, "Who are the monsters?"

Are they the characters who look different, whether by having vampire teeth, three boobs or profusive facial growths? We meet a bunch of them quickly, as Leonard assembles them as a team. Even Auguste, and his short assistant Goliath, have huge and pointy noses.

Or, as Leonard suggests, are they the people who attend the circus he sets up for them all to perform in? He wants the world to see them as special because of their talents, though it's far more likely that they'll see them as special because of their physical differences. To solve that problem, he has a plan and we see it put into motion at the very first performance.

Of course, the reaction isn't positive, with a set of common responses, some merely louder in their proclamations than others. "They are so ugly." "Go home, freaks!" "I came to see a show, not a circus of horrors."

So Leonard ends the show right there, with a refund for everyone. However, he keeps the three loudest objectors behind, ostensibly for a private show, something never before seen, but really to burst a vial of chemicals in front of them that transforms them each into one of the monsters they so hate.

Will grows horns like a goat. Helena sprouts a full beard and moustache. Edgar Finnigan is given psoriasis on the cheeks. However, this is not permanent, Leonard is keen to point out. The effect will only last as long as their hateful attitudes persist and will vanish if they come to accept the performers as just people.

Of course, how they react to that affects the direction of the story, so Will and Helena stay and become part of the troupe, the former as a knife thrower and the latter demonstrating an affinity for aerial silk dancing. Edgar Finnigan, on the other hand, storms out, attempting to return to his previous life as a powerful lawyer but failing because nobody wants him with his new disfigurement.

How well Leonard's plan will work depends on how things proceed from there. How many audience members will he need to transform before a diminished local population comes to accept a circus of skilled performers instead of the freakshow they initially see? Will that ever happen? Will those transformed find a way to change and so transform back? Will the people rise up against a circus that's building a troupe by transforming its audience? Will love win or hate? This film asks a lot of questions but it's also happy to provide answers. And, of course, to find out what they are, you'll need to watch *Monstrus Circus*, as I'm not going to tell you.

What I will tell you is that the film looks like a million bucks. The locations are all fabulous, whether we're talking the historical buildings in Reims and elsewhere in France, or the wild countryside of Scotland; the circus itself is on a small promontory into a loch. The actors are able to fit perfectly into those backdrops, with strong assistance from excellent costumes and excellent make-up effects.

The script is also happy to take its time but never for too long, a steady progression taking us exactly where we need to go. Auguste sets us in motion at the very outset by asking that first question and we gradually realise why he did so. We also find ourselves so engrossed in the story and its expanding cast of characters that we forget to ask a relatively unimportant question of our own, namely why the circus is located in Scotland. When the script answers that question, we both laugh and roll our eyes because it's funny but also unimportant. I still remember the ALIFFF audience responding to that audibly when I first screened it, as it was also a submission to my full film festival.

Now, had that been the ultimate point of a thirty minute film, it would have been a clear letdown, but it isn't. The point is that question that Auguste asked us. Who are the monsters? The way the film answers that is not a letdown in the slightest. The entire story answers that and in multiple ways, because, of course, there is no simple answer. If there was, many of the world's problems could be easily solved using a vial of Leonard's transformation formula.

The ultimate success of *Monstrus Circus* is a natural extension of that question. While it's easy to read Auguste as asking only within the context of this film, having us answer for each of the many characters we're about to see, it's fair to say that he's asking us about ourselves too and the people around us in real life.

Are we the monsters? What would our take on these characters be should they be there as entertainers in front of us instead of this film? Would we be an appreciative audience, seeing them for their talents alone? Would we be like Will and Helena, outwardly hateful but open to a potential for change? Or would we be like Edgar Finnigan, consumed by our hate?

And, eventually, we realise that the formula Leonard uses is just a visual aid. If we despise people for being different, then we are already ugly, whatever we happen to look like.

This is a very easy film to watch, but it asks a lot and hopefully we take some of that away with us. That's great filmmaking.

All together: "Bienvenue, Monstrus Circus!"

MONTY AND THE RUNAWAY FURNACE (2016)

DIRECTOR: JOE TARANTO
WRITER: AMANDA STEINHOFF AND JOE TARANTO, BASED ON A STORY BY JOE TARANTO
STARS: CHARLIE DIERKOP, ERIK PASSOJA, MARISSA TAIT AND BIFF WIFF

Often steampunk films are genre films, with the genre itself up for grabs. So far, I've talked about science fiction, romance, musical, urban fantasy, horror, comedy... and sometimes they simply happen to be period pieces. This short film, which I was amazed to discover was part of what Joe Taranto needed to create to finish his Master of Fine Arts degree, so technically making this a student project, is a decent old fashioned feelgood story.

The Monty of the title is Monty Montyson, a workman who looks after the heating system at VinTucket Industries. The runaway furnace is G.R.A.C., which is the heart of that system, a huge chunk of red metal that's appropriately anthropomorphic given that Monty is able to understand her, as if she's talking to him, and she him in return. He's scratched an E on its plaque because she's a kind of replacement for his dead wife, Grace. And I do realise that I've already given it a gender, because Monty has.

Both Monty and G.R.A.C. have clearly been serving VinTucket Industries for ever, but that sort of consistency isn't reflected upstairs in the boardroom. Walter VinTucket II used to be the boss but he's gone now and his son, Walter VinTucket III, is clearing house, right down to a portrait of his father that's been there for so long that his image has almost become part of the stone behind it. The one thing he can't get rid of is Julie, his father's secretary, because that was prohibited in his will.

I've seen a lot of student films in my time. I've even judged student film competitions in both Arizona and New Mexico. Some are awful and some are magnificent, but they tend to be cast with students and teachers, few of whom are really actors. Occasionally, a student had a slice of ambition or a teacher had contacts and someone professional joined a cast, a scenario perhaps more likely in Los Angeles, where Joe Taranto was at Loyola Marymount University. And, if a student is good enough, they can get a seriously good performance out of that pro.

I may never have seen another student film that was better cast than this one. It's not just that Taranto got stars into his project, it's that he got the right stars into the right roles in his project and directed them to stellar showings.

Monty is Charlie Dierkop, who isn't a huge name but is a highly talented actor who you've likely seen before and more than once. Maybe *The Sting? Butch Cassidy and the Sundance Kid?* The TV show *Police Woman?* He was even the killer Santa in *Silent Night, Deadly Night.* He's an absolute joy in this film, at the age of eighty, a worthy lead character indeed.

Another couple of working actors who give fantastic performances here are Erik Passoja and Marissa Tait.

The former is a prolific voice actor, but he couldn't be a better physical actor than he is here playing Walter VinTucket III. Walter is an asshole and I'm sure Passoja isn't, but he does an amazing job at playing one. He's also very good indeed at playing a paranoid asshole on his last nerve, which is good because it doesn't take long for him to have to pull that skill out of his toolbox and gradually escalate it as the film runs on.

The latter is almost the opposite as Julie, his secretary. She's charmingly nervous and very old fashioned, dressed like she's Amish and a mere glimpse of skin below the neck might be enough to make her have a fainting spell. She has power, though, however reticent she is to use it and she's delightfully apologetic when she does. In some ways, she's as much a heart and soul to the building as G.R.A.C.

There is a fourth face you might recognise, that of Biff Wiff, which neatly shows up three times at once, playing each of the characterful Borises, who run a company that Walter II had refused to do business with but Walter III is eager to quickly invite in for a joint project.

The story is pretty simple and it's not really about VinTucket Industries in the slightest. It has everything to do with Monty and his wife Grace. They loved each other dearly but she's clearly passed and he clearly hasn't got over it yet. She was his favourite singer and he puts a record of hers onto his gramophone turntable at the very start of the film. We hear it too, but it doesn't play because the device is broken. It plays in his head because he knows it by heart and we hear it that way.

Now that she's gone, he cares for the other Grace, namely G.R.A.C., the furnace. He hears her sing too and dances with her to the music that she makes. We hear that song as well, in the neat rhythms of cogs, steam and pistons, a sort of Victorian industrial music.

The catch is that Walter VinTucket III hears it too, up in the boardroom and he's not a fan.

He wants the noise stopped and that escalates over time to wanting the furnace gone. And, in a highly emotional scene, it goes, but G.R.A.C. turns into Grace first in Monty's mind, which isn't the last connection between the two that the film has to show us.

Of course, that means this is fundamentally about change and that's why the rest of what we see, with Walter and Julie and the Borises, not to forget the ghost of Walter II, who may or may not exist only in his son's mind, just as G.R.A.C. housing a sentient being who's hardly pleased with the job the new boss is doing so far with his inheritance may or may not truly be there either. Our brain says that it isn't. Our heart says of course she is. Duh.

Watching *Monty and the Runaway Furnace* for this project is my first viewing in a long time. I heard about this film long before I saw it, as it was making serious waves on the film festival circuit. It didn't play ALIFFF but it did play at a number of other festivals I'm aware of and it won a few awards, including one here in state at the Arizona International Film Festival, for Visual Storytelling. I'm sure it would have won more but it's over half an hour long and what I said about film festivals and long shorts in my chapter about *Creatures of Whitechapel* holds as true here as it did there.

What I learned this time through is that it's as powerful now as when I first saw it and on each occasion I've screened it, which has been twice thus far. It would have been three, but it was approved for an Academy qualifying run and that temporarily limited my permission to screen it. That's a good way to underline how good it is though. Not a lot of films get to that point and this one absolutely deserved such an honour, even if it didn't land a nomination at the end of it.

MORGAN AND DESTINY'S ELEVENTEENTH DATE: THE ZEPPELIN ZOO (2010)

DIRECTOR: REGULARJOE

WRITER: METAPHOREST

STARS: JOSEPH GORDON-LEVITT, LEXY HULME, LAWRIE BREWSTER AND CHANNING TATUM

Here's a short film that needs some serious introduction, because it doesn't look or sound like anything you have likely ever seen before, even though you're absolutely going to know a couple of faces.

The first name to know is HitRECord, which began as a hobby for Hollywood actor Joseph Gordon-Levitt in 2005, then as a professional collaborative platform in 2010, where anyone could contribute to shared creations. Its first project was a short film, *Morgan M. Morgansen's Date with Destiny*, but it's released animations, music videos, books, albums, art, you name it.

That first film is a fantastic introduction to their collaborative process, rather fortuitously because this film is a sequel to it.

It began as a piece of writing, by Sarah Daly using her community handle of Metaphorest. It's in English but not quite. Most of the words are transformed into some alternate universe version of English, always following the rules of the language but never in the way that we do, not now and not ever, unless we translate it poorly into Chinese then challenge Google Translate to translate it back. It's unique and it's very deliberately done with overkill.

So, for instance, Destiny naturally prepares for her date by putting on make-up, but that's described as "her headfront was polly-painted with fauxface, lips cherried to the max." Think about that and imagine it expanded across six frantic minutes of narrated storytelling.

Gordon-Levitt, as RegularJoe, recorded it as a voiceover. HitRECord collaborators drew the imagery they saw in the words. Those images were animated by others. Gordon-Levitt acted it out with Lexy Hulme, against a pure white backdrop. Lawrie Brewster filled empty space with visuals. Someone created a score. Many others performed it. In the end, a hundred and eighty different people from around the globe, most of whom had never met, had teamed up to create a short film to play at Sundance.

It's a thoroughly original piece of art, both in how it was made and in how it plays. I'd be rather effusive about it, except that, the same year, HitRECord released a sequel, namely this film, and it's better again in every way.

In that first film, Morgan and Destiny have their first date. It doesn't start well, as Morgan orders the rabbit and Destiny's vegetarian, but he covers it and eats salad with her, so it gets a lot better, enough that he almost lovesplurts later with butterflation.

Fast forward to this film and they hold their eleventeenth date on the Zeppelin Zoo, which is exactly that, a zoo maintained on a zeppelin, which is whisking through the sheeny cobaltic blue-fest high up-top the big smoke. They've come a long way past mere restaurants now.

Unfortunately, there are two obstacles that manifest to stand in between this passion-pair and a wonderful eleventeenth date.

The first is a tragedous wrong-hap. Madame Balloffur, a pamperfied purr-pet that Destiny has perhaps ill-advisedly bag-hidden within a paw-pouch, goes cat-about. Naturally, Morgan is tasked with locating and retrieving her, not an easy challenge, given that she's snuggled in under the enormo-paw of the big-maned purr-beast in its bar-box.

In other words, Destiny's cat has jumped out of her handbag and snuck into the lion's cage, with Morgan tasked with getting her back.

If that wasn't enough, just as he's trying to accomplish that, he's faced with the cognified, smarmarific lothoriator, Lionel, in the bulked-up Victorian circus strongman form of Magic Mike himself, Channing Tatum, who we're told is Destiny's pre-now love-buddy. And Lionel is burning for a fight with his replacement.

Fortunately for Morgan, the food penguin is here. On that first date, he was just a waiter in a tux. On this one, he's got a new job, working in the rare-bears treat buggy, costumed as a monochromic rare-bear, and he plays an even more crucial role in how well this date ends.

By the way, I hope you're following along in the absence of visual explanation, but, if not, he's wearing a black and white panda mascot costume. Why? Because the Zeppelin Zoo is an experience and that's apparently the uniform when working concessions by the pandas.

As you might imagine, it's a lot easier to get what's going on when you can see it, which is why this was made as a short film rather than simply published as a piece of nonsense poetry that isn't really either. However, the words, as narrated by Joseph Gordon-Levitt, a star in the previous century and even more so now, are an intrinsic part of this experience. And it is an experience, as much as a film. It's likely to overwhelm you but also entertain you enough that you watch again and realise what these folk are actually doing. Deciphering the rapid-fire narration is half the fun.

I have no idea if Gordon-Levitt saw this as a steampunk short film in 2010. In many ways, it isn't. However, in many ways it is, because the word salad that he delivers feels highly retro-futuristic, perhaps something put together by a Victorian antecedent of J. G. Ballard's, who was attempting to create futuristic slang.

The setting fits too, as a zoo on a zeppelin is a neatly alliterative steampunk idea, with a lot of Victorian visuals: monocled rats in top hats and tails, straight out of cabinets of curiosity; ornate architecture including spiral staircases; bare knuckle boxers settling it like men; even a shot of H. P. Lovecraft, if I'm not mistaken.

Sure, Destiny's dress would be a scandal at a Victorian society party, but both Morgan's and Lionel's outfits would fit in well, as would both of their moustaches and their fight scene too.

So I'm happy to call this a steampunk short film, merely a particularly unique one. It may help a little to see *Morgan M. Morgansen's Date with Destiny* first, but you don't have to. Suffice it to say that they had a date and it went well enough that they had more of them and this eleventeenth one on the Zeppelin Zoo merely happens to be the most memorable. Join them on that one or this, it doesn't really matter. I'd merely suggest that, if you're going to seek out both, then watch the first first and the second second, because this is a step up in every way.

So, slap your seeglobes around this, folks!

THE MYSTERIOUS GEOGRAPHIC EXPLORATIONS OF JASPER MORELLO (2005)

DIRECTOR: ANTHONY LUCAS

WRITER: MARK SHIRRELS

STARS: JOEL EDGERTON, HELMUT BAKAITIS, TOMMY DYSART AND JUDE BEAUMONT

The oldest film in this zine, *Jasper Morello* is also one of the most acclaimed, with a host of awards to its name, even if it failed to add the Academy Award for Best Animated Short Film to its tally, losing, with Shane Acker's *9*, to *The Moon and the Son: An Imagined Conversation*. The winner featured the voices of Eli Wallach and John Turturro; this one boasts Joel Edgerton in the same year he returned to play Owen Lars a second time in *Star Wars: Episode III - Revenge of the Sith*.

He gives voice to the titular Jasper Morello, which means that he also narrates this entire twenty-six minute film, chronicling a voyage into the uncharted waters of a strange world, first on the *Resolution* and, after that wrecks by crashing into an abandoned fishing vessel in a storm, on that ship instead.

I don't know that his entire world falls into the definition of steampunk but the city state of Gothia does and that's where we begin. It's Morello's home too and, when he embarks on this new assignment, as the navigator on the *Resolution*, he leaves his wife Amelia behind in a plague-stricken city. It's clearly well known for its Victorian industrial landscape, all cogs, wheels and steam, but it's becoming equally as known for the disease that's ravaging it.

Whether the Republic of Laurencia follows suit, in either way, we don't know, but Gothia trades with it and the *Resolution* is tasked with deploying wireless communication beacons to the trade routes between them. As they go, an unexpected passenger, Dr. Claude Belgon, has authority to conduct experiments on the crew in order to see if elevation might be a cure for the plague, based on a flimsy observation that airmen don't tend to catch it.

That's the grounding here, also noting that Morello is lucky to have work because, on his previous trip out, also as a navigator under the same captain, Otto Griswald, he made an error that caused a man's death. Chekhov's Gun says that will have further meaning to come.

Jasper Morello looks wonderful today in 2024, but it's tough to imagine how groundbreaking it must have seemed back in 2005. Steampunk had been around a long while but the general public had no idea what it was. If anyone had even heard the word, they likely associated it with a certain brand of fiction or perhaps that infamous feature version of *Wild Wild West*.

The look is based in silhouette, which is why *The Adventures of Prince Achmed* is so often cited as an influence, along with wayang, a form of shadowplay puppet theatre that's a traditional artform in Indonesia. This is different, though, not pure 2D silhouette work like I talked about in my chapter on *Invention of Love*.

It's mostly 2D, albeit done in layers, and that

work is physically achieved. However, there's movement in three dimensions too, entirely computer generated. Scenes unfolding behind the silhouettes may be painted but sometimes are digitally animated, with clouds added for effect throughout.

The colour palette is interesting too, as it's a primarily monochrome look, whether sepia or a different colour for a different scene that's a heavy reminder of the hand tinting that went on back in the silent era. However, there is an occasional use of colour, sparingly done and in most instances representing the plague. Those with the disease appear in silhouette, but the plague itself in more vibrant colour.

It's a fantastic look that hasn't been copied much in the almost two decades since, even as other films have taken a similarly silhouette-based approach to their animation styles, not least *Invention of Love* and *The Last Fairy*.

It's worth noting that both those films, and this one, are dark in theme. We start with the title character tormented by his past failure, a career ender that somehow doesn't do that. As he leaves, we learn how Gothia is stricken with the plague and people are dying in scores. The journey has nothing to do with that, but by an opportune coincidence, stumbles upon a cure.

They've been blown off course by a fourteen day storm and been forced to transfer over to the fishing vessel, but Morello is doing his job and getting them back to the trade routes. An island appears out of the clouds and it's on the island that they discover a monstrous creature that they kill and eat. The ship's cook, LeBrun, has contracted the plague, but broth from this creature miraculously cures him. Even at this point, however, things are not remotely happy because of aspects I'm not going to tell you, as you absolutely should seek this picture out for

yourself and see where it goes.

What I'll add, because it's no spoiler, is that this works well as a standalone film, beginning and ending in appropriate places. However, it wasn't intended to be the one and only *Jasper Morello* film. Wikipedia lists three further films that were supposed to follow, suggesting that all three of them—*Jasper Morello and the Return of Claude Belgon*, *Jasper Morello and the Ghost of ALTO MEA* and *Jasper Morello and the Ebenezer of Gothia*—would be feature films.

I can't find a citation for that online, but the film's director, Anthony Lucas, did state on a steampunk forum in 2009 that Mark Shirrefs, the film's writer, had completed two scripts to continue the story. They went down well with the various production companies but SBS, the Special Broadcasting Service, which existed in Australia from 1994 to 2007 as a multicultural public broadcaster, declined to be involved. He didn't say that there were four films, whether they would be features or shorts or what they were to be called, so maybe he expanded on it somewhere else I can't see. Any which way, it was clearly intended to continue the story.

Frankly, it doesn't matter, but the way this builds its world is immersive. We want to see more of Gothia, hopefully after the plague has been vanquished, and we want to see the rest of the world, not just Laurencia but all of it. If this one city state is so richly drawn, even in silhouette, surely we'd be in for a treat on the further voyages. As it hasn't happened so far, I seriously doubt it'll get picked up again, but a comic book or a novel would be welcome.

I'd even settle for an underground mash up with another franchise, perhaps *Jasper Morello and the Prisoner of Azkaban* or *Jasper Morello and the Temple of Doom*. Where do I sign up?

NEMO (2014)

DIRECTOR: NICOLAS CHATTOU-COUMBIL

WRITER: NICOLAS CHATTOU-COUMBIL

STARS: JULIEN DOUYÈRE, ARIANE GREMIGNI, MAXIME PATTERI, JEAN CHRISTOPHE FURGONI, DENIS MORGE AND DENIS-CHARLES HERRMANN

Here's another steampunk short film that I discovered long before I watched, because the version online had no subtitles. Unlike *Eugen*, it's dialogue driven and so didn't make a lot of sense to anyone not fluent in French.

After a few years, not seeing any change, I reached out to the filmmakers who sent me a copy of the script in French. I threw that into Google Translate in sections, then tweaked the rest into something that made coherent sense. And all was right with the world!

Well, not quite. My paltry understanding of French meant that I found myself completely stuck about three quarters of the way through and couldn't finish the job. Luckily, someone else was able to do that, so I could discover how it all ends.

That said, how it ends was the only thing I knew coming in, as the short is called *Nemo* for a reason and that reason wasn't hard to figure out. It's the back story that Jules Verne missed out of *Twenty Thousand Leagues under the Sea* as a way to keep his famous captain firmly a man of mystery. He made certain hints and he also fleshed them out in *The Mysterious Island*, but it seems to me that Nicolas Chattou-Coumbil, as writer, chose to ignore the latter book entirely to fill in the blanks left in the former afresh.

Oddly, given how the film is structured with a reveal at the end that Hashti Sarai, who has been our lead for almost forty minutes, will be henceforth known as Nemo, it fells like telling you that is a spoiler, but it isn't. If we failed to pick up on the very name of the film, it begins with a quote from Jules Verne, explaining that "The world does not need new continents. It needs new Men." Naturally, the man in a film called Nemo who meets that need is going to be Nemo, even if he's introduced to us at the very outset as Hashti Sarai, a young boy with brown skin who's clearly inquisitive.

What's more, if we have any familiarity with *Twenty Thousand Leagues*, the way this moves is totally in keeping with what we know. Captain Nemo valued freedom above all and he has an especial disdain for colonialism. And so young Hashti grows up working in a factory, in parts unknown, for a colonialist regime that clearly represents both France and Britain.

He first impresses Lord Greylight, who runs the factory named for him, and, while he talks in French, he feels English. After Hashti saves the factory in the the chief engineer's absence, Greylight becomes the boy's champion, taking him to the governor to talk up his knowledge and his ingenuity. Society isn't impressed and the Countess, who is exquisitely French, treats him as a curiosity. "Ah, a learned monkey" she tells him to his face when she learns that he's able to read. The governor himself sometimes feels French and sometimes English. All speak French, so maybe I'm reaching here.

The sides are set pretty clearly early on. The hero of the story, who becomes an anti-hero, is Hashti Sarai, a brilliant young engineer who understands the systems he sees and has solid ideas about how to improve them. His partner is Lord Greylight, who's not purely a good guy but certainly leans towards it. He takes Hashti under his wing and allows him not only to talk about his ideas but to implement them. He's a strong voice of support every time something has to be escalated up to the governor, who is the ultimate owner of the factory, potentially on behalf of the French Republic. However, he does what he's told, which causes a clash, and it's telling that he doesn't seem to notice that the boy he presents to society wears no shoes.

While the colonialists generally serve as the bad guys, it's surprisingly the Countess who is chief among them. The governor is on her side for sure, but is a little more open to benefits a bright young boy might bring financially, just so long as he doesn't get too big for his boots.

And that's a crucial note, because there's an additional level here that's been floating since the very beginning. There's a precedent here. Hashti Sarai is the way he is through genetics, because his father was highly talented too and even worked alongside the previous governor to do much of what he's trying to do now. The experiment did not end well and the Countess is wary of repeating it. And that's almost fair enough, though that's only ever part of it and keeping the workers in ignorance so they can't see how they're being exploited is another.

There's also a wildcard, called Le Surin. We know nothing about him until very late in the film, but he waltzes into the Countess's place almost halfway into the film as if he owns the place, armed guard in tow. That guard forcibly steals a highly talented pianist in a red corset

too, so there's power being wielded. We don't know what or how or why and where the film goes only adds depth to Le Surin.

There's a lot to like here, though it's obvious that not everyone acting in this film is actually an actor. Julien Douyere has his moments as Hashti Sarai, but it's Ariane Gremigni, playing the Countess, and Denis-Charles Herrmann, as Le Surin, who are clearly the strongest actors. The former has quite a few credits, albeit in an array of short films, while the latter seems to have done nothing else, at least according to IMDb, which fails to list most of the cast.

None of the acting is bad, so if I were to call out a negative, it would be the way the film is broken up into a number of delineated scenes, each with its own title card and text, the latter of which is often narrated. There isn't a reason for this, as far as I can tell, as we would be able to keep up throughout without those breaks. So Scene 4 Part 1 becomes Scene 4 Part 2? We don't care. We do care that we move from the characters over here to those over there, but we're already aware of that without help.

Some might grouse, I guess, about the film being almost forty minutes long, but I get that. There's a lot of character building here and a good progression of story. The talky scenes do not dominate and there are action scenes too, here and there, as needed. There's also plenty of industrial backdrop but gorgeous landscape too. The grotto on the Countess's estate is *très bon*, even if her little library there comprises an array of actual steampunk books, like *The Steampunk Bible* by Jeff Vandermeer, in French; *Les magiciens du fer* by Cetrix and Yuio; and an RPG book called *Château Falkenstein: aventures épiques à l'ère de la vapeur*, or *Castle Falkenstein*.

What matters is that it gets to where it must and it does it with character.

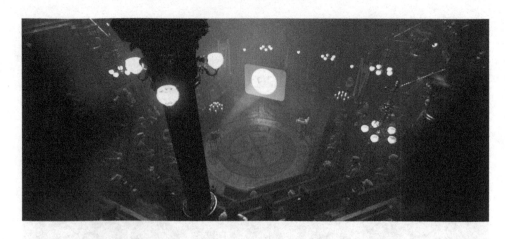

THE NINGYO (2017)

DIRECTOR: MIGUEL ORTEGA

WRITER: MIGUEL ORTEGA, TRAN MA AND GREGORY COLLINS, BASED ON A STORY BY MIGUEL ORTEGA AND TRAN MA

STARS: RODRIGO LOPRESTI, TAMLYN TOMITA, JERRY LACY, GABE FAZIO, MALI MATSUDA AND LOUIS CHANGCHIEN

I like and recommend every film included in this zine and I'd go a lot further than that on a lot of them. If you twisted my arm, though, to persuade me into calling out a favourite, then it would be this one. That's why you're getting two extra pages of screenshots when no other film in the zine does. I simply couldn't narrow the choice down to six images.

It was submitted to ALIFFF, my film festival, in its second year, 2017, and it blew me away. I deliberately bring in judges to choose all my short film award winners, and change them up every year to keep fresh perspectives. I always have the audience choose my feature winner. But I reserve an award for myself to give out, a Festival Director's Award, for any reason I like. I suspected that it would be my choice for that year by the halfway mark and I knew for sure by the end. And, even though I screened many amazing films that year, it was indeed.

That's because the wonder it holds goes a long way beyond anything just cinematic to be a celebration of life. It's one of a mere handful of films that literally awes me every time I see it. I can't watch without tearing up, because it carries that much of an impact, not just on the first majestic viewing but, crucially, on every further viewing too, even though we know the wonders awaiting us around the next corner.

It's a period piece and that period is a little newer than steampunk tends to require, most of the action taking place in 1911. However, it speaks very much to the Victorian era and the attitudes it held. The breathtaking footage as Marlowe makes his way underground to visit H. Prestor Sealous represents the biggest and most impressive cabinet of curiosity I've ever witnessed. And everything fits the mindset of steampunk perfectly, the pride in creating art that's functional for everyday purposes, from the oaken furnishings housing the exhibits in the Field Museum to the mere box containing the gift Sealous sends Marlowe to entice him into that visit. The detail here is impeccable, right down to wax seals on letters and tattoos on the chests of dying men in kitchens.

What's most impressive is that most of what we see doesn't exist. While this film looks like a million bucks and could have been made by a Hollywood studio, should one choose to make a period adventure about cryptozoology that's partly told in Japanese with authentically cast ethnic actors, it was in reality a labour of love by husband and wife Miguel Ortega and Tran Ma, with their team over a period of time.

You aren't likely to believe this if you watch the film or if you just dive into the screenshots on these pages, but most of it was shot inside their house with a crew that rarely exceeded four. They built sets there, incorporated what antiques they could find on Craigslist, and did everything they could to optimise the budget, which was raised on Kickstarter, 1,025 backers contributing just over $80,000. This does not, I will hammer home to you, look like $80,000. It looks like ten or twenty times that, but it was made by two amazingly talented visual artists who could bring to this personal project what skills they wield in their day jobs.

Ortega has a bunch of credits on films that you've seen, doing model and texture work for CafeFX, Tippett Studio and others. How about *Silent Hill*, *300* or *Night at the Museum*? Maybe a couple of *Twilight* movies, *Thor* or *Red Cliff*. Ma has worked for CafeFX too and Digital Domain, doing model and texture work on films such as *Nim's Island*, *Speed Racer* and *Red Cliff*, *G. I. Joe: The Rise of Cobra*, *Transformers: Dark of the Moon* and *Alice in Wonderland*. Those pay the bills but thoroughly original films like this one and *The Voice in the Hollow*, a seventies-style claymation voiced in Swahili that tells a Faustian story of two young sisters, are clearly what they want to do and I couldn't be happier.

This film follows Chris Marlowe, an explorer known for discovering the okapi, previously a myth, "the African unicorn". There's a gallery named for him in the Field Museum but he has fallen out of favour there, for two reasons.

One is that he's now looking into mythical aquatic creatures such as the melusine, undine and, most especially, the ningyo, the Japanese mermaid. Legend says that ningyo flesh, when consumed, has healing properties and endows near immortality. He's even found a map that might lead to the ningyo. Of course, the dean doesn't want him to propagate pseudoscience but he gives a presentation anyway, seeking a backer for his proposed expedition.

The other is that, while he's renowned as a hunter, bringing back priceless specimens for the museum, he's changed his ways. He wants to stop killing these creatures in order to give them posterity in displays, in favour of finding a way to conserve them alive and in their own habitats. A colleague asks whether, if he wants to preserve the ningyo, then wouldn't proving its existence be the worst thing he could do? A thesis could be written on that subject alone.

Of course, the map to the ningyo becomes a MacGuffin, a host of characters seeking it. One is Sealous, who sends a skull of a melusine as an incentive to visit. There's also Kiyohime, a Japanese lady whose clan works to protect the ningyo, because her mother accidentally killed one centuries ago and the land paid the price for ten generations while she watched all her descendants grow old and die. The museum's interest isn't entirely clear either while others undefined to us are in on the quest too.

These conflicts aren't resolved here, as this is a proof of concept short film with a feature version potentially in the works, but there is a resolution of sorts in what Marlowe discovers when he visits Sealous and how he reacts to an impressive proposition. The film stands whole even if there's also much more story to come, should that feature indeed be made.

And I just can't talk up Sealous's collection enough. It has to be seen to be believed, quite literally, but also from our perspective as mere filmgoers. If there's a set in film I want to visit more than this one, I can't name it and yet it's not real, most of it amazingly generated by the magic of what Ortega and Ma do for a living.

I haven't mentioned actors. Tamlyn Tomita is reason enough to watch a film and she puts all her nuance on show here. Jerry Lacy, who was Bogart in *Play It Again, Sam* is exquisite. All the elements fall together. Watch this. Now.

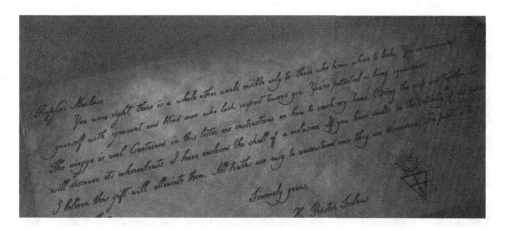

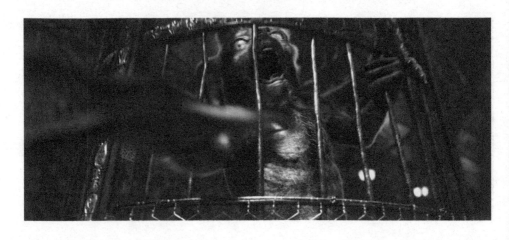

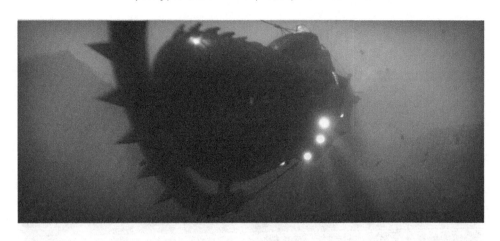

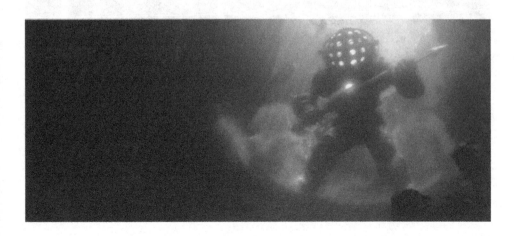

RUBY'S SKIN (2014)

DIRECTOR: CLAIRE TAILYOUR

WRITER: CLAIRE TAILYOUR

STARS: OLIVIA COOKE AND JOHN BOWE

"Let's start at the end," says Ruby and so we find ourselves with her in an otherwise empty ballroom at the Langham Hotel, London. It's 1865, the door is barred with a broom and her father is trying to get in. She's worried about her memory being flawed, that there are lots of moments but nothing in between them. It's a good setup, because there are a whole lot of possibilities about what's behind this and we'll soon jump back fifty-five minutes to find out.

She's a lovely young lady who has quite the character, as we see when the first hydraulic lift in England starts to rise, with her in it. Her father is also there, taking copious notes and annoying the operator with his questions that cover topics he can't answer. Meanwhile, Ruby balances a nest of Matroshka dolls on her head and absorbs the moment.

She's played by Olivia Cooke, who was not a major name at the time, even though she had started a long run in the TV show *Bates Motel*. Her first features came in 2014, the same year as this, but it was 2015 when she gained major attention for playing the dying girl in *Me and Earl and the Dying Girl*. That sparked major film roles, including one in a gothic with appeal to steampunks, *The Limehouse Golem*, and the lead female role in Steven Spielberg's *Ready Player One*. By 2018, if not before, she was a big star.

Her father here doesn't seem to care. He has some sort of mechanical device to feed him as he writes at their table in the hotel restaurant, which leaves him no time whatsoever to talk to her. The wait staff notice and gossip about them. She notices too and asks questions. Why don't you talk to me? Do you love me? When's my birthday?

And that's where things get weird, because, when pressed for answers, her father gives an answer that doesn't work for her at all. "That's incorrect," she tells him. Last year, he told her different, the conversation promptly spins out of control and then off she runs to get us back where we started.

Now, there are hints here. Of course, when he gives his explanation to Ruby and us both, it prominently features the Matroshka dolls as a metaphor. He emphasises her importance to him: "You are the most important thing in my life, that I promise." But he's clearly a scientist and he sees the world as "a revolution of cogs and steel". What's more, when he knocks over a glass of water in his frustration and it drips onto her chest, a burn mark manifests on her shirt, the final trigger for her to run.

Put it all together and it shouldn't surprise too much when he explains, but there are still nuances and touches that make it all the more poignant. While it might not seem it initially, this is a highly emotional short film, stuffing rather a lot of impact into a running time that falls just under thirteen minutes, fewer if we consider that most of it bursts out during the film's finalé. It's in the revelations, the reason for them and the meaning they carry.

Interestingly, much of the emotional weight is carried not by Ruby, though Olivia Cooke is excellent in the part even this early in her film career, but by her father, who I don't believe is ever named but is credited as Derby.

The actor is John Bowe, far more established in 2014 than his now more famous co-star. I've seen him on the big screen in the Bond movie *The Living Daylights* and on the small screen in a whole slew of British TV shows, albeit none of the ones that made him best known to the majority of the country. He'd appeared in two hundred and fifty episodes of England's most popular soap opera, *Coronation Street*, previous to this and was just beginning a four hundred and nine episode run on another major soap, *Emmerdale Farm*.

He's very good indeed here, most obviously because he's not sympathetic in the slightest as the film begins. He's a pest to those around him, like the elevator operator, and he ignores his daughter, unwilling and perhaps unable to answer her questions, so blustering excuses at her until she shuts up. Which she doesn't.

He gains our sympathy late in the film, after we've already taken Ruby's side, even without knowing what sides mean in this context. It's fair to say that Cooke makes Ruby delightfully characterful and we can't help but wonder if something is wrong for her father to ignore so much charm right there in front of his eyes. So it's all the more powerful when Bowe waltzes up when we least expect it to almost demand our sympathy and get it without us having an expectation of giving it. Tellingly, he doesn't take it from his daughter. He expands it over to him too and that's stellar work from Bowe.

I don't want to give everything away here, though I can't resist including the screenshot at the top of the page opposite because it's the most steampunk moment in the film, so I kind of have, but there's more to it than that. I have not stripped the pleasure of this film from you before you've even seen it, unless you've seen it already because you were there when I put it front of new eyeballs at steampunk cons.

Nobody lets the side down here, but I ought to mention Claire Tailyour here, because this is her film more than it's anyone else's, even if they happen to be more famous then or now. She produced it, she wrote it and she directed it. She also edited it, which was a particularly important role in this film, because it relies on momentum and poor editing would break it in ways that even a good director might struggle to fix. That she was both helps, but it's edited with panache. I have lots of respect for editors who do superb jobs without most people even noticing that they did anything.

I want to talk more about where it goes but I can't without really venturing into the sort of spoiler territory I'm only skirting a little close right now. What I can say is that where it ends up prompts us to reevaluate everything that's already done and so it's a prime candidate for immediately watching again.

In my book reviews, there are occasionally titles that don't just impress me but do so in a way that I want to chat about with others, so suggest that they would be magnificent book club choices. If you can imagine an equivalent for short films, this would qualify as one that I'd recommend to the club and look forward to chatting about with everyone else.

How about you watch it and then we'll chat!

S.P.A.G.H.E.T.T.-1 (2009)

DIRECTOR: ADAM VARNEY
WRITERS: ADAM VARNEY AND KYLE ARRINGTON
STARS: JOSHUA MIKEL, TIM NETTLES AND MARK MARPLE

Here's a short film I encountered in 2010, as I was discovering what steampunk was. I saw it first at a local film festival, chosen by author Michael Stackpole for a Sci-Fi Shorts set at the International Horror & Sci-Fi Film Festival.

Back then, the festival happened in the run-up to Halloween, in mid-October, a slot which my film festival, ALIFFF, would later inherit, so I'd already attended Steampunk Street in Mesa earlier in the year and met so many people in the local scene who changed my life. I started to list them here and it took over the page, so I hope they all know who they are. Thank you.

All of which is a less long winded way than it was of saying that I saw *S.P.A.G.H.E.T.T.-1* as a sci-fi short, but I knew that it was steampunk. It checks all the boxes that steampunks hold dear: a period setting that promises alternate history shenanigans; an eccentric madman; an unlikely steam-powered scientific gadget; and a whole heck of a lot of fun. Authentic horse-drawn carriages serve as a welcome bonus.

It's an American Civil War story, but told in the south, where the local population of Ideal, Georgia, clearly considers it a War of Northern Aggression. It's told by Dr. Sinclair Tyler, who we first encounter leaping off a roof in blood-stained full body underwear. As odd as it may seem, he's the good guy.

Tyler used to live in Ideal when apprenticed to Prof. Arthur Couch, but he moved north to study medicine while Couch remained in the south during a "shall we say, heated climate." Yes, the American Civil War. Fast forward to a year after it ended, 1866, and Couch's heart is apparently failing, so he's requested that Tyler visit to fit him with a new invention he's built that will save his life.

You won't be surprised to find that this new invention is the S.P.A.G.H.E.T.T.-1, but Couch is reticent to explain what that means, which isn't the first red flag we see. However, he gets Tyler to operate anyway, inserting two hollow iron poles through his abdominal cavity, so as to hold a pair of magnetic prongs, to which an accessible control console will be attached.

It's only as Tyler is cleaning up after surgery that he sees Couch's poorly burned documents in the front yard, which conveniently reveal a sinister plan in cartoon fashion: everything is successfully burned except for the three steps he'll follow and the conclusion.

And, while this is shot entirely live action, a little effects work added so the invention will work for us, it really is a live action cartoon. It takes no imagination to translate this into the sort of adventure that we might expect from Warner Brothers in a *Looney Tunes* short. Some scenes almost scream live action cartoon and the way that both the lead actors overact their performances is very deliberate indeed.

I won't spoil what Couch's plan is, though it is well telegraphed throughout, so revelation is only a surprise to Tyler. However, I have to explain what S.P.A.G.H.E.T.T.-1 stands for. I'd be a serious tease if I didn't do that, especially as this is one of the few short films in this zine that you can't wander over to your browser to watch online.

So I'll take a breath and reel off what this crazy acronym stands for. S.P.A.G.H.E.T.T.-1 is a Steam-Powered Anti-Gravitational Hydraulic Energy Transference Transport. "One," as the lunatic professor adds cheerfully, as he looks over his shoulder at Tyler with his remaining good eye. Of course he wears an eye patch and walks with a cane. Why wouldn't he?

I should explain here that, like *Monty and the Runaway Furnace*, this is another student film, made at university as part of a degree. In this instance, the school is Florida State University whose College of Motion Picture, Television & Recording Arts generated a lot of film festival submissions that I've thoroughly enjoyed over the years. They do good work there.

I'm assuming that Adam Varney, the film's director and one of its writers, was a student there, but he's gone on to be an editor for TV, with a long list of credits, and a producer of an array of TV prank shows. I'm assuming as well that Joshua Mikel, who plays Tyler, was also a student there. He's continued as an actor and may be best known today for eleven episodes of *The Walking Dead*, as one of its most twisted and despicable characters, one redditor calling the Savior "a peerless and wholly unmitigated bucket of puke". Interestingly, another says he tends to be typecast in that sort of role, which is completely unlike that of Sinclair Tyler.

Tim Nettles brings flamboyant life to Couch, revelling in his performance as he gives it, but he's older, I think, and has remained acting in short films, so I'd guess he was a actor in the local amateur scene who lent his talents to the university for films like this, as I presume was Mark A. Marple, who's the other actor tasked with playing a named character, the effusively moustachioed Gen. Joshua Chamberlain.

As you might imagine, a live action cartoon that tells a story focused on the American Civil War needs to get its humour right. While any film inherently has potential to go horribly off course in a long list of ways, this one utterly relies on its script.

Put simply, if the acting or the camerawork or the effects were less effective, then the film would follow suit but it would probably still be a lot of fun. If the script went wrong, then the film would be a disaster and that seems all the more applicable now in 2024, fifteen strange years after it was made.

The good news is that the script is probably the best aspect of the film. So it functions on cartoon logic? That's fine. What matters is the way that it places this live action cartoon in a southern town one year after the Confederacy lost the war, meaning that the "shall we say, heated climate" may have cooled a little but not a lot and the local population is very wary indeed whenever a visiting Yankee moves too close to a Confederate cutlass.

Fortunately, the script walks the line well, even with its Yankee hero and its Confederate villain. It has absolutely no intention to touch on anything political, why the war happened and why it ended. It's all about one madman in isolation. The film wraps up with a handshake too, which is crucial. It doesn't mean that this newfound peace will hold for ever, but it does mean that it will hold for now and with a little more emphasis than it did before we began on that rooftop with Dr. Tyler about to jump.

If you can find it, watch it. It's wonderful.

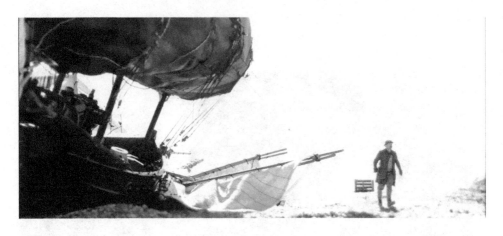

STEAMWRECKED (2014)

DIRECTOR: CHRISTOPHER MATISTA
WRITER: RACHEL HEMSLEY
STARS: SARAH BOOTH AND TIM HILDEBRAND

This is another student project, but I was in a good position to watch this one progress, as it was more local. *S.P.A.G.H.E.T.T.-1* was shot in Thomasville, Georgia by film school students based in Tallahassee, Florida. *Steamwrecked* is a California production, made as a senior thesis at the Dodge College of Film and Media Arts at Chapman University in Orange and shot in the memorable landscape of the California desert.

If memory serves, I heard about the film as a sort of aside. We were at a Gaslight Gathering, now Gaslight Steampunk Expo, in San Diego, where I regularly present Roadshow sets, but we were about to head home for Arizona. Our final stop before the car was Operations, so we could say goodbye to friends there who work and run that convention and one mentioned that there was a panel just a couple of doors up about a steampunk film, in what must have been the last programming slot of the con. Of course I went straight there and that's where I learned about this.

They hadn't shot the film at that point and I think they were pushing their Kickstarter as a means to raise money for costumes, props and effects work. I was impressed by Chris Matista, the director, and Rachel Hemsley, the writer, both painfully young but also eager and very clearly driven to produce a quality short film. I kept in touch with Chris who kindly gave me permission to screen a completed film at some events, including a later Gaslight. He's become a regular there, albeit as a photographer not a filmmaker, documenting events with style.

To be brutally honest, there's not a lot here but that's because they kept it simple and put their efforts into making what they did count. That's not a bad approach for a filmmaker and it paid dividends here, because what we see is good and what we leave with is emotional and impactful. It's a solid slice of life in a particular steampunk universe and it would be easy for it to be expanded, whether through other short films or through comic books or novels.

The basic concept is that the world still runs on steam but lightning is a powerful source of energy and ships can harvest bolts to confine inside portable canisters and transport back to civilisation. As you might imagine, it's a highly dangerous business, even after the storms that prompt their livelihood have dissipated.

And we see the results immediately, because we open with August and Rowe surrounded by the wreckage of their ship. The credits give us their full names—August Morlock and Rowe Windsor—but what matters is that it's his ship but she has a vested interest in the delivery of its lightning canisters, of which two appear to have survived the crash.

This prompts an immediate conflict because there are scavengers in the area, reminiscent of Tusken Raiders in *Star Wars* and they're just as dangerous. August is aware that scavengers weaponise lightning, if canisters fall into their hands, and use it to down other ships. And so he has to release the valuable lightning there and then, to adhere to protocol. Rowe refuses to let him do that and even pulls a gun on him to prevent him from doing so. That's a simple but highly effective method of telling us there is a story here and Sarah Booth's performance tells us that we want to know what it is.

There's not a lot more to tell, but I ought to add that a scavenger scout attack sprains one of Rowe's ankles, so she doesn't have a simple trek ahead of her. Even so, they set out on foot because they don't have any other option, and they carry the two canisters with them.

It's a little bit talky and there are a couple of montage scenes of them walking, but none of that impacts the pace much and Hemsley has a few details in hand to release when she needs to keep us going. And so these characters build as they walk and deal with scavengers until we get to where we're going.

There are also a few little details that I must call out for special mention.

One is that the first montage scene, which is the longer of the two, doesn't drag because of the way that it's edited. Sure, the backdrops of huge residual boulders (like you, I learned that term from *Tremors*) help to keep it all visually interesting, and Matista wisely keeps our leads in long shot or out of frame entirely, but I love how one vista is faded slowly into another to give an impression of time passing. The editor was Scott Coleman, who's editing in television nowadays, even if not on anything I've seen.

Another is the fact that the night time scene appears to be shot by firelight and that's very evocative. I'm sure there were lights and other equipment to ensure that we could see all that we need to see, but it feels like we're sharing a flickering fire by the rocks with the characters

and that makes it feel all the more personal as their stories start to unfold.

A third is that, during that firelight scene, a ship appears, hardly visible in the dark sky but a huge beacon of hope nonetheless. That hope is quickly dashed with some neat effects work, but I have to admire how ambitious this scene is. I remember working with Chris to optimise the projector I had to use at Gaslight, because its bulb wasn't the brightest, and it still didn't quite do the job. This shot needs to be seen in the right conditions: a dark room with quality equipment, so that you can just about see the ship until, wow, you absolutely see the ship, at least for a little while.

There are films that start out with a lot but don't do much with it. That tends to increase our disappointment, because our expectations are high and the delivery is low. It's far better to go the opposite way, especially if you don't have a large budget or a large crew. This cost about $20,000 of Kickstarter money and Chris Matista knew exactly where it could be put to good use. So it didn't have a lot, but he and his crew did a lot with it, and that's impressive.

It probably helped that he was able to cast a couple of actors, both Canadian, who may not be names we recognise but are professionals who do solid work. There are a lot of them in California but it always helps to cast the right ones. They did here and both Tim Hildebrand and especially Sarah Booth bring a lot of depth to relatively straightforward characters.

I'm not sure where you can see this online, but it certainly made it to Amazon Prime at a point in time. Maybe it's still there.

TEA TIME (2014)

DIRECTOR: J. DEREK HOWARD
WRITER: J. DEREK HOWARD
STARS: ERIN HECKEL, WILLIAM GANTT AND ADRIELLE PERKINS

It's well known in steampunk circles that we should always stop for tea, but it's rarely been quite so frustrating as in this short, which was funded through Kickstarter for a mere $3,000 and shot over two days at the historic Samuel Culbertson Mansion bed and breakfast, located in Louisville, Kentucky.

This provides a neat link to actual Victorian fiction, because, as you might imagine, it was the home of Samuel Culbertson, the President and later Chairman of the Board of Churchill Downs, the home of the Kentucky Derby. The family became the basis for the fifteen book series of *Little Colonel* stories by Annie Fellows Johnston. His sons, Craig and William, became Keith and Malcolm, or *The Two Little Knights of Kentucky*, the titular characters of the second volume in the series.

I haven't read those books, but I have seen and enjoyed this film, shot in their house. Like *Steamwrecked*, it hardly boasts a complex story, but it's a funny and eventually very satisfying one, with a glorious last line.

The star of the show is Elizabeth Brown, the mad scientist of the household, to the abiding disappointment of her Aunt Judith, who is the perfect Victorian lady, keen only to marry her niece off to an appropriate suitor. We can tell that, however much she loves her, she sees it as the only hope Elizabeth has.

Elizabeth, on the other hand, has plans. Lots of plans. She simply aches to be an inventor, a respectable profession in her day, and all that needs is one worthy invention sent off to the Inventor's Institute. And, as her first words in this film suggest, "At last, it works!"

I'm a little shocked to find, even a decade on from this short, none of the actors have done much of anything else in film. I wouldn't claim that Erin Heckel is the greatest actress in the history of cinema, but she's a joy here, even in a role that's deeper than it had any right to be. I can't conjure up even one negative aspect to her performance, even if she's an amateur. I'd suggest that her enthusiasm is infectious. She may have invented something ridiculous, but I left the film with the wish to invent something of my own, even if that's ridiculous too.

We don't see this new invention, but we do see others, including the one she uses to keep a sort of video diary that allows us to follow on with her progress. Of course, there isn't a heck of a lot of progress. She excitedly sends off her invention, using a male pseudonym, naturally, that of Jules Burroughs. Ha. And she waits.

And waits. And waits. And waits. Eventually a reply comes in and we watch poor Elizabeth run through all of the stages of grief in quick succession. She quietly comments, "A simple no would have sufficed," but relishes when the anger arrives and she swears revenge on one George Caldwell, rejector of her genius.

And, just as we're caught up in her maniacal charm, Aunt Judith informs her that she must stop for tea. It's a fantastic way to change tone on the turn of a dime, as Elizabeth transforms from a wannabe inventor to a young lady who must attend the suitor who's calling on her. It doesn't start well, but it deteriorates from that until an absolutely explosive conclusion. And that final sadly accepting line from her Aunt Judith is utterly priceless.

I won't spoil where it goes, though it hardly ought to surprise much, given that there are a mere three characters in the film and only two locations: downstairs in Elizabeth's laboratory and upstairs in Aunt Judith's front room.

What I will say is that it goes there well with a host of little moments that shine.

Many of them are comedic jabs at the social niceties of Victorian etiquette. It's clear to us that Elizabeth knows them but doesn't care to follow them and that extrapolates to who she is, what she does and her ambitions about who she wants to be. While she's clearly shown as a mad scientist, it's fair to say that much of her madness is simply daring to do what she aches to do, regardless of what society might have to say about her gender. And while Aunt Judith is likely to disagree with us, we can't find a fault in Elizabeth's mindset because we don't live in her world and don't want to.

Steampunk, after all, isn't about us living in the Victorian era, it's about rewinding history to the Victorian era, then making all the right changes and none of the wrong ones. We're on the mad scientist's side here.

I particularly love how that entire mindset, about which entire novels have been written, is also condensed here magnificently into two separate sounds. When Elizabeth changes into appropriate attire to meet a suitor, she gasps audibly as her corset is cinched in tight. When she switches back into far more comfortable attire, albeit still quintessentially steampunk, she lets out a similarly audible sigh, exhaling in luxurious comfort. She can literally breathe again. A hundred years of change is condensed into a gasp and and a satisfied sigh.

Another fabulous touch, that was unneeded but is very welcome, arrives when we see the business card of Elizabeth's suitor. I won't tell you his name and I won't share an image of it, just in case you haven't figured that out, but I will say that it is very neatly animated. There's an Inventor's Institute logo, of course, and it's an animated one, even on a physical business card. There are animated cutaways on a pair of corners too that I swear every steampunk I know, including me, would fight a duel for. The only flaw is some truly awful kerning; where is that apostrophe supposed to be? The placement of an apostrophe on a business card bearing no importance to the script at large is hardly an major flaw to a short film, of course.

At the end of the day, the worst thing about this film is that it ends, which is always a good thing to say about a short. However, that's just because we're having so much fun with these characters. There's no reason for the story to keep going, so it doesn't.

The only thing that writer, director, editor, cinematographer, producer and probably the teapot heater upper, J. Derek Howard, possibly could have added is a static coda telling us the future for these characters, in the style of the *Hot for Teacher* video, say, or *National Lampoon's Animal House*. That's because, even in a skimpy eight and a half minutes, Elizabeth Brown was richly defined for me and I want to know how she ends up.

So, answers on the back of a postcard to the usual address, please!

TOPSY MCGEE VS. THE SKY PIRATES (2014)

DIRECTOR: TRAVIS STEVENS
WRITER: YURI LOWENTHAL AND TARA PLATT
STARS: TARA PLATT, YURI LOWENTHAL AND JOHN DE LANCIE

Here's another steampunk film featuring an array of major names, but these are mostly not ones you'll recognise. The creators of the film are Yuri Lowenthal and Tara Platt, a massively prolific husband and wife team of voice actors who literally wrote the book on the subject.

In 2004, they founded their own production company, Monkey Kingdom Productions, and this is one of a number of short films they shot under that banner. They naturally brought in a lot of colleagues, people like Taliesin Jaffe as prolific in the voice acting world as they are, but a host of others that I presume are friends.

What's notable is that a bunch of these folk have acted in other steampunk films or shows, so I have to presume that they're fans here too and they're simply doing what they enjoy.

Lowenthal himself is in the first episode of the long awaited *Hullabaloo* series of animated films, which I'll be screening in the Roadshow at Wild Wild West Steampunk Convention 12, at which I'll be launching this zine. Californian fan supreme and noted maker Shawn Crosby is also in *Love in the Age of Steam*. John de Lancie is the infamous Q from the *Star Trek* universe, but he was also Janos Bartok, the Nikola Tesla character in the steampunk TV show *Legend*.

It has to be said up front that this is not the sort of slick and detailed production that, say, *The Ningyo* is. This is good old fashioned pulp adventure and it's unashamed to look as cheap as it does because it's all fun. On the outside,

all these ships are obviously models, but they all look very cool anyway. Inside, they're made of patchwork wood, metal and cardboard, and obviously so, but the action doesn't slow down long enough for us to pay too much attention.

And there's plenty of action, some of which would normally benefit from a lot of carefully added post-production. For instance, there's a scene where Topsy McGee takes down a pirate with twin swords, but they have to be the least effective killing blows I've ever seen. It's more like she's wiping his blood off the blades onto his trousers, but there isn't any blood, as that would usually have been added in post too.

It sounds like I'm being overly critical, but my point is that it's not remotely ashamed of looking cheap and it works anyway. This is the sort of thing we got in old school pulp serials back in the forties and this is pretty authentic. It's merely set a little further back in time, as a steampunk adventure demands.

We see the date of 1877 on the copy of *The Argus* that Mr. Pepper is reading. That's John De Lancie's character, whose primary job is to reenforce to Topsy that the sky is no place for a woman. That's a repeated mantra here that a slew of characters bring up, but usually right before she kicks their asses.

There's a neat homage early on that's hard to catch because it's so fleeting, but it's telling. She's Tara Pratt, of course, playing the titular Topsy McGee, and she's stuck waiting at home in a sepia-toned silent film prologue for word of her husband, Sean, in the suitably dashing form of Yuri Lowenthal, who's out battling sky pirates. However, the headline on the *Argus* is now "Courageous Captain Captured", so it's up to her to head off into the sky to rescue him, taking for inspiration the book she's reading.

The homage is the book, *Mistress Branican* by Jules Verne, which is anachronistic because it wasn't published until 1891 but is appropriate here because it's about the heroine of the title launching an expedition to search for Captain Branican, her husband, in the Australian bush, after he's reported lost at sea and presumed to be dead. Verne based it in part on the real case of Lady Franklin, who led a search for Sir John Franklin, her explorer husband, who was lost in the Northwest Passage.

It's when Topsy decides to buck up and head out after him, whatever Mr. Pepper might say about it, that we shift into widescreen colour. It's a neat touch to highlight that she's moved forward in time just by making that decision and film technology really ought to match her.

There's not much to the story at all, but it's always fun, whether she's trying to source her ship from sky rats in a back alley ("The sky is no place for a woman.") or fighting pirates on board the one she obtains, taking on a massive black pirate and a sexy romance cover pirate ("You have spirit. But the sky is no place for a woman.") Almost as much as *Tea Time*, this is a strongly reaffirming film for kickass women in waiting and, I should add, men comfortable in their masculinity, who have no problem with women kicking ass and taking names, because why should it only be their job?

It's not difficult to imagine how it ends and you'd be absolutely right. I can't spoil how she gets her husband back, because we don't see it,

but she does and that relegates Mr. Pepper to the couch while she plays Sean at chess. When the military folk arrive with a new mission, it's both of them who stand up to prepare to meet it and that's how it should be.

I haven't seen enough of Lowenthal to state whether he should do more physical acting or whether he should stay in voice acting, where he's an absolute legend. He's not in this film at all long enough to judge, but he looks the part for sure, whether in sepia or colour. This isn't his film, after all; it's his wife's.

And Pratt, however much we don't buy into certain finishing moves, does great here. She's also a legendary voice actor but she works this film physically and shines with both facial and body movement. Sure, she's a very still young lady in her Victorian reading outfit early on in the film, but that's a glorious steampunk fight suit she puts on when we leap into colour and she throws herself into the role. She looks fine in the outfit at the end too, but it's not a patch on the other one.

De Lancie is one of my favourite actors, who has never seen a scene that he isn't happy to steal, but he gets very little to do here. Crosby gets more, but he's content to be background for Pratt to fight through. It's always her film.

Just as Topsy McGee sits at home waiting for her husband to come home, I've been waiting for a long while for the superhero craze to end and it hasn't happened yet. With phases being popularised like "superhero fatigue", maybe it will come to pass, but the natural replacement in my eyes is old fashioned pulp adventure. It works for Indiana Jones and it should work for others too. And when it gets here, I hope these two majorly connected talents pitch a Topsy McGee feature film because I'd be queueing up for it and I wouldn't be alone.

THE UNUSUAL INVENTIONS OF HENRY CAVENDISH (2005)

DIRECTOR: ANDREW LEGGE

WRITERS: ISAAC CAVENDISH AND HERBERT CARLSON

STARS: HUGH O'CONOR , FIONA O'SHAUGHNESSY, SHAUN BOYLAN AND FRANK KELLY

While some steampunk filmmakers remain with the genre, I've only included two films by the same director once in this zine and that's *The Unusual Inventions of Henry Cavendish* and *The Girl with the Mechanical Maiden*, both films directed by Andrew Legge.

Both are highly worthy but I've never been able to choose between the two, favouring one over the other this month but then the other way next. This was the first of them, released in 2005, eight years ahead of its successor.

Maybe *Mechanical Maiden* is more emotional but this is a more authentic silent film, free of accompanying sound effects. People don't talk here because we can buy into the technology needed for sound film not existing yet; they don't talk in the other because they just don't. The same applies to colour and widescreen, as that film looks like a modern film, merely with no dialogue, while this one looks in every way like it could believably have been made in the early 1920s. And yes, it feels weird to realise I can't merely say "twenties" any more, because we happen to be in another iteration.

It's also perfectly cast, with Hugh O'Conor, a criminally underknown Irish actor, able both to clearly channel Charlie Chaplin and yet still make the role of Henry Cavendish his own. His admiration here goes to Fiona O'Shaughnessy as Miss Catherine Palmerston, and she's highly expressive, truly lighting up in his presence as a woman in love might. I've seen both before in roles utterly unlike these.

The story will seem familiar because it was recycled in much simplified fashion in Italy as *The Craftsman*. While that was streamlined into under seven minutes, this breathes for almost sixteen with levels that simply didn't make it into the Italian film, released nine years later.

Henry Cavendish is a young inventor, living in Dublin in 1895 where he's testing his latest invention in the street when a beautiful young lady passes in a carriage and they both fall in love. They're going in opposite directions, she one way down the street and he the other on a primitive Segway with no control stick, so that he floats past almost like a vision.

He crashes into a newsstand, so captured by this vision of loveliness, but the newspaper he catches has her photo on it. It seems a rich industrialist will be holding a garden party in honour of his daughter. It's her, of course, and her name is Catherine. This is masterful stuff, a complex scene distilled down to its essence and presented in a sublime artistic way.

That newspaper piece also says that suitors should each bring a gift; rather than buy one, this creative genius builds one. It's not exactly the flowering metal plant built by his Italian equivalent in *The Craftsman*, but it looks rather similar. And so he dresses up and joins the line by the maze behind the sprawling Palmerston estate, right behind the villain.

In case we didn't recognise the silent movie context clues in his thick moustache, foul look and constant cigar smoking, his hissing name is the Honorable Salacious St. John Somerfield Smythe. S. S. S. Smythe. It's clear that he'd be up for a bit of posh, but wants her money too. Shaun Boylan is tasked with playing more of a one note character, so there's less depth there to be had but he does a good job nonetheless.

Having a serious rival for the lady's hand is one level present here that didn't make it into *The Craftsman*, but there's also a bigger one. A lit cigar butt dropped maliciously by Smythe onto Cavendish's mechanical device causes an explosion and that sets history on a particular path, one that doesn't work for either Henry or Catherine. So what's an inventor to do, but figure out a way to fix it? And how can you fix something that's already happened?

It seems a little odd to compare this film to *Mechanical Maiden*, because they do what they do in very different ways. That felt like a more modern film, maybe from the seventies, which looked back at the Universal horrors for some influence. This feels like a classic film, made in that era, part *City Lights* and part *Modern Times*.

However, there are definitely comparisons to be made, beyond the fact that neither uses spoken speech as we expect it today: one uses intertitles; the other deems it unimportant.

Both stories revolve around inventors, with a sampling of their creations in active use in the film. Here, that doesn't just mean the one he presents to Miss Catherine. It also means a contraption to remove his hat and place it on the hatstand, an automated showering device and the very crucial pedal-powered invention

pictured opposite that does what I'm sure you have figured out simply has to be done.

The two films have significant crossover in cast and crew, because Legge clearly keeps the same people around him where possible. Even those who didn't work on both films did on an array of other Legge films. The lady in the suit of the mechanical maiden, Serena Brabazon, is here too but in a less obvious role.

And both heavily rely on period visuals, in part through historic Irish architecture. When we see Palmerston's estate, it's the Kilruddery House and Gardens in Bray. The prison, from the outside and perhaps from the inside, is the Kilmainham Gaol in Dublin. Drimnagh Castle is here somewhere too, possibly as the home of the Smythes halfway through. This makes the film feel authentic, something that steampunk films often struggle with, not having access to this sort of history.

One thing I'd praise here but not in the later film is the intertitles, which were designed by Christine Ellison. I don't just mean the words, which are succinct and appropriate, or indeed the typeface used, which is elegant. I mean the understanding that intertitles don't have to all look the same. Ellison chooses to craft ornate chapter headings and plays with emphasis as Smythe smears Cavendish's name during the aftermath to the explosion. It's good work.

Another is the score by Jürgen Simpson, as it serves a very different purpose to the one in *Mechanical Maiden*. That, by Liam Bates, was an orchestral score that had to be built around an array of sound effects and a general ambience, because we could hear the film. Its job was to accentuate rather than replace. Simpson has full reign to replace, and so composed a piano score that underpins mood. It's good work too.

But really, just watch both films. Trust me.

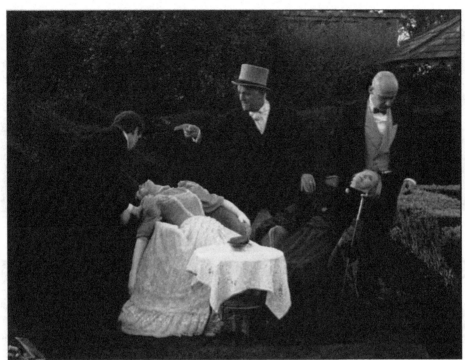

VALIANT (2014)

DIRECTOR: ROBIN PHILLIPS

WRITERS: ROBIN PHILLIPS, SCOTT BABA AND AND JONATHAN EDWARD MILLER, BASED ON A STORY BY ROBIN PHILLIPS AND SCOTT BABA

STARS: GIL DARNELL, JASON HICE, ANDREW VARENHORST, DANIELLE PARKER, ALEXANDER MCCONELL AND DAVID SAJADI WITH NAVID NEGHABAN AND CAMDEN TOY

Here's another film that you can't see online but which may well get there at some point, as it began life as another student film; it simply grew beyond it. Originally, it was a thesis film, made at the University of Southern California, but its success there led Robin Phillips to build it into something more, so he used Kickstarter to raise another $16,000 to enhance it.

I haven't seen the student film, but I found out about this one early because the costume designer is Nola Yergen, who was arguably the first Arizona steampunk most people ever saw, courtesy of her appearance in the steampunk episode of *Castle*. She does amazing work and I was thankful when she put me in touch with Phillips, who gave me permission to screen his film at Wild Wild West Con in 2014. I was able to thank him in person when it got accepted at the International Horror & Sci-Fi Film Festival and screened there in 2015 with him present.

It calls itself a steampunk action adventure, which is pretty accurate. Even though much of it probably counts as dieselpunk rather than a strict definition of steampunk, there are still a lot of airships here and the mindset matches a lot closer than in, say, *The Wars of Other Men*, a more overtly dieselpunk short that would still be of interest to steampunks.

Valiant is the name of an aeroplane, stolen and flown by a trio called the Valiant Three, a trio whose bounty is quickly increased early in the film to £400,000. That's in pounds, because the balance of power in this world is between England and the Danish Empire, who fight for control of New Paris, naturally in New France, which sprawls above the Prussian Kingdom. In charge of England is the elderly but spry King Mortimer, whose sworn enemy is Harald, the Emperor of Denmark.

We'll meet Mortimer soon enough, but this film kicks off with the Valiant Three winning a bar fight. They're led by Ronnie Amberson, an Australian; Fred the pilot is clearly continental and possibly French (or New French); while an impeccably characterful Shorty is a Scot. None are English, but England is where they happen to be right now.

The bar fight may have begun over the fact that one of the King's Guard was there and, as he dies, custody of the young girl he was with falls inherently to the Valiant Three. She says she's Emily but so's her doll, so that isn't much help. All we know for sure is that she's highly important to someone and that someone turns out to be King Mortimer.

There's a lot of easy influence to see in this film, but it's never derivative. It's more *Firefly* than *Star Wars* or *Indiana Jones*, but they're all there and we can certainly hear John Williams cues in the score by Jeremy Tisser. Really, it's just a story that sits in that sort of genre, as an action adventure: some theft, some smuggling, some doing what's right in the face of evil, and all of it needing fists and guns and explosions.

I've seen Gil Darnell in both film and TV, but without really knowing who he was until this film, because he's a quietly effective Ronnie in charge of the Valiant and its crew. It's what he says that goes and the others trust him. Fred is Andrew Varenhorst, also quietly capable and a trustworthy sidekick. It's Jason Hice who stirs up situations as Shorty, because he's a hotshot wildcard who likely sleeps with his large gun and is always ready to use it. He's responsible for comic relief, but he's also clearly capable.

Because this isn't a Hollywood feature, they all appear as grimy as they would be in reality, not neglectful of their appearance but covered in the detritus of their jobs: bruises, engine oil and good old fashioned sweat. They look good and Yergen's costumes make them look better still. They are costumes, of course, but they're so natural that we don't even acknowledge it. We could totally believe that these three were pilots and smugglers who just waltzed into the casting office and looked the part already.

The overt costume is King Mortimer's, as he has every intention of looking better than any other character just because he's the king. He struts around in the overt trappings of power just like he's a banana republic dictator, crown on his head and medals all over his chest. The actor is Camden Toy, who you've seen before.

Of course, the Valiant Three end up facing a huge airship with massive guns, so are forced into landing wherever they're told, which, you won't be shocked to discover, is exactly where King Mortimer is, because he wants Emily. The surprise is that they're welcomed, £400,000 on their heads or not, and a dinner is thrown for them and a newfound alliance they somehow forged. Shortly steals the cutlery.

I hope this finds its way online so that it can continue to be seen, now its film festival run is long over. There are few flaws—some obvious rear projection work evident and the length of the end credits being painfully long—so we're able to settle down and just plain enjoy this. It is full of wonderful characters, good and bad, who work hard with or against each other to make the whole thing good old fashioned fun.

I'd watch a feature film set in this world and I'd watch a TV show too. Movie serials haven't been made for a long time now, but that would be the perfect format for this sort of thing. It's good comic book material too, because it must have an overtly visual focus.

The point is that, while we're given a story to follow and it does what it needs to do to tell that, it's abundantly clear that there are other, just as worthy stories to be told in this world. What's next for the Valiant Three? Does little Emily get home? How is the balance of power altered by what happens here? The answers to all these questions should be found in the next thrilling episode of *Valiant*, if only Phillips was willing to make one. Instead, it looks like he's gone into visual effects, perhaps inspired by a string of miniatures and digital effects in this short film, provided by people with day jobs in that sort of thing in Hollywood.

I talked about pulp stories taking back over from superhero stories in my chapter on *Topsy McGee vs. The Sky Pirates*. That was fun too, but a lot less substantial than this. They share the same mindset, though this doesn't have such a feminist outlook. If you liked that film, as you should if you're reading this, then you'll adore this one. It's twenty-four minutes full of pulp goodness (plus six more of credits).

WIDDERSHINS (2018)

DIRECTOR: SIMON P. BIGGS

WRITER: SIMON P. BIGGS

STARS: BRIAN COX AND JAM GRAY

I've talked here and there in this zine about how many professional actors and Hollywood stars have appeared in steampunk short films, as it's a shockingly big number. I haven't even mentioned my biggest Roadshow coup, which was *Cowboys & Engines* at Wild Wild West Con 4, as that screening was the world première of a Malcolm McDowell film, a dream scenario for me. However, that's less a short film and more a collection of scenes from a feature as a proof of concept, a feature left unfinished after the death of its driving force, Richard Hatch.

This animated film from Scotland, however, features another huge name, one that to me is the biggest star covered in this book, because the voice of the unnamed lead character here (the credits simply call him Mr. Widdershins) belongs to Brian Cox, my Hannibal Lecktor.

He's a dour soul, partly because he has to be as a Scot and partly because he's fed up with a revolutionary device that has taken the world by storm, whichever world that happens to be. The billboards outside, carried by dirigibles of some description, talks up a perfect world, one where "steam-powered innovation anticipates every whim". It's a ball that floats in the air and does everything, with a lens eye and a pair of articulated limbs.

That means that every morning, he's woken up on time by a device that triggers music on a gramophone, opens the curtains, shaves him, smooths his hair and even trims his eyebrows.

That's before he opens his eyes. It also dresses him, collapses his bed into storage and serves him breakfast. He hates every moment, all the way to the daily positive outlook message.

I don't know what this marvel of steampunk efficiency is officially called, but he names his Bertie and it does everything for him. It's like Clippy if it actually worked and did everything before you even asked for it. It really is like an efficient human butler with a tiny moustache.

The suggestion, once we leave his house and see what goes on elsewhere, is that everyone's lives are being run by these devices. And that leans into complete uniformity. Everyone lives in the same style of multi-storey terraces and rides to work in the same carriages. They may well all wear identical Victorian businessman suits, with bow ties and top hats. There isn't a jot of originality left anywhere in the world.

Except his same ol' same ol' rut is suddenly interrupted by someone riding a flying device, defacing that billboard with guerrilla graffiti, transforming "Hello perfect world" into just "Hellworld" and our grumpy protagonist is on board with everything about that, leaning out of his carriage window to shout "Bravo!"

If he's impressed at the one individual we've seen, he's more than impressed when he sees that it's a woman. He's in love. And now we're off and running, because he would dearly like to meet her and will do whatever it takes to do that. Bertie, of course, doesn't want to help in the slightest and so turns off his alarm clock.

I loved everything about this short, which I first saw screening at the International Horror & Sci-Fi Film Festival. It's animated but not in a style I'd seen in film before, not drawn quite so much as it's engraved. Everything looks like the sort of illustrations in *The Strand* and other Victorian or early 20th century periodicals, an ironic comment given that I believe it was all done digitally, making it technically CGI.

The look is a huge part of why it succeeds so well. That it's done well may actually function as a secondary aspect to the fact that it's such a unique vision. To see anything even similar, I'd have to dive into foreign animation, which I guess this is to Americans. There might be a film or two somewhat like it made somewhere on the continent, say, in eastern Europe.

I love that it's hard to even identify a genre. Of course it's steampunk, given that it exists in a world with a steam-powered revolution, but it isn't remotely like any other steampunk film I've seen, including the others in this zine. It's an animation too, of course, and a short film, a pairing that gives IMDb safe classification. It's satire, I guess, done with neat comedic timing. It's drama, it's dystopian, it's retro-futuristic. It's horror, in its way, at least to me, because a world of uniformity scares the crap out of me. Ultimately, I guess, it's a romance.

So it stands unique, which I appreciate. The next successful aspect is what Cox brings to it with his voice, because he's a real character in this film, but not so much that he has a simple ride. He's already elevated above the norm as someone who hates the predictability of it all and the uniformity, but he doesn't fight it too hard. He accepts it and grouses about it, as if it would magically change anything. Crucially, at a particular moment in the film where he has

the opportunity to change everything, he gets it horribly wrong and apparently scuppers the one chance he had. Cox sells all of this, and he sells the eventual happy ending too. Bravo!

He's not the only voice actor in the film, the rogue aviatrix and graffiti artist given voice by Jam Gray, about whom I know precisely nada. The character is Miss Caprice, again according to the credits, because she's not given a name in the film itself, but she's Jam Gray's only role at IMDb. She doesn't get much to do here but she does it capably enough. It keeps her firmly at a distance for a reason and that has nothing to do with her talent.

The final contributor I'll call out for special mention is Giles Lamb, who composed a score that's infectiously vibrant. Everything's built on rhythm, because this world is built just the same, but it's done more with xylophones and brass punctuation than drums. It goes where the story needs to, but it's a perky earworm of a score with simple riffs that are now well and truly stuck in my brain once more.

At the end of the day, of course, what abides the longest from *Widdershins* is its message, to embrace the different, if not perhaps quite so literally as this gentleman would like to, but in everything we do. Just because everyone else uses this particular device (which makes it an obvious metaphor for a smartphone), doesn't mean we should and we might be missing out on a lot if we do.

And, really, in a film zine about steampunk, a genre that used to be underground for a long time before a few celebrities co-opted it and turned it into a brief fad, that's appropriate. To create a steampunk film is a labour of love and the thirty examples covered in this zine are all worth checking out for that reason and also for all the others you've read here.

WHERE TO SEE THESE FILMS

Here are urls to help you find these films online, both informationally at IMDb and to watch, at either Vimeo or YouTube. These links were valid at the time of publication but may change over time, so if you can't find something at these links, search for it instead. It may have moved.

1873: The Insidious Intrigue
https://www.imdb.com/title/tt3453134/
https://vimeo.com/106792317

The Anachronism
https://www.imdb.com/title/tt1478346/
https://vimeo.com/11034820

Bill & Maggie's Intergalactic Taxi Service
https://www.imdb.com/title/tt6058450/
https://www.youtube.com/watch?v=i33QjmJjkSA

Corset
https://www.imdb.com/title/tt5662926/
not viewable online

The Craftsman
not on IMDb
https://www.youtube.com/watch?v=GkN9MYJwWjU

Creatures of Whitechapel
https://www.imdb.com/title/tt5038306/
https://www.youtube.com/watch?v=wcPHc8h_198

Della Mortika: Carousel of Shame
https://www.imdb.com/title/tt4270750/
https://www.youtube.com/watch?v=2Hm78oF2HAg

Dr. Grordbort Presents: The Deadliest Game
https://www.imdb.com/title/tt2287709/
https://www.youtube.com/watch?v=OSwNFVjCquU

Entre les Lignes
not on IMDb
https://www.youtube.com/watch?v=TBLMzSOQV3Q

Eugen: The Steampunk Musical
https://www.imdb.com/title/tt3259376/
https://www.youtube.com/watch?v=qAh2vsZjRYE

A Gentleman's Duel
https://www.imdb.com/title/tt1159650/
https://vimeo.com/8379529

The Girl with the Mechanical Maiden
https://www.imdb.com/title/tt2066112/
https://vimeo.com/52082549

Invention of Love
https://www.imdb.com/title/tt2104922/
https://www.youtube.com/watch?v=PTdzCAGH3lU

The Last Eagle
not on IMDb
https://vimeo.com/286486647

Mask of Vengeance
https://www.imdb.com/title/tt5573936/
https://www.youtube.com/watch?v=EH4ATUhpJlY

The Mechanical Grave
https://www.imdb.com/title/tt2055773/
not viewable online

Monstrus Circus
https://www.imdb.com/title/tt10408092/
https://www.youtube.com/watch?v=ME6_F6aRtIw

Monty and the Runaway Furnace
https://www.imdb.com/title/tt5109178/
not viewable online

Morgan and Destiny's Eleventeenth Date: The Zeppelin Zoo
https://www.imdb.com/title/tt1640152/
https://www.youtube.com/watch?v=EshILeABbHw

The Mysterious Explorations of Jasper Morello
https://www.imdb.com/title/tt0469146/
https://vimeo.com/29517738

Nemo
https://www.imdb.com/title/tt5932514/
https://www.youtube.com/watch?v=bZPK6H9MkH4

The Ningyo
https://www.imdb.com/title/tt3899676/
https://vimeo.com/244707785

Ruby's Skin
https://www.imdb.com/title/tt3159546/
https://vimeo.com/77575022

S.P.A.G.H.E.T.T.-1
https://www.imdb.com/title/tt1543772/
not viewable online

Steamwrecked
https://www.imdb.com/title/tt7108168/
not viewable online

Tea Time
https://www.imdb.com/title/tt3654912/
https://www.youtube.com/watch?v=TZa4Dh_Ay9A

Topsy McGee vs. The Sky Pirates
https://www.imdb.com/title/tt3497232/
https://www.youtube.com/watch?v=U6x3MU-b7dk

The Unusual Inventions of Henry Cavendish
https://www.imdb.com/title/tt0463388/
https://www.youtube.com/watch?v=v0-fHZnfcxM

Valiant
https://www.imdb.com/title/tt2584842/
not viewable online

Widdershins
https://www.imdb.com/title/tt8496784/
https://www.youtube.com/watch?v=nWORBZIEjbI

SUBMISSIONS

I welcome submissions to Apocalypse Later Music, though I can't guarantee that everything submitted will be reviewed.

Please read the following important notes before submitting anything.

I primarily review the good stuff. There's just too much of it out there nowadays to waste any time reviewing the bad stuff. Almost everything that I review is, in my opinion, either good or interesting and, hopefully, both. I believe that it's worth listening to and I recommend it to some degree, if it happens to be your sort of thing. Now, if you're a die hard black/death metalhead, you might not dig any of the psychedelic rock and vice versa. However, maybe you will! Open ears, open minds and all that.

I have zero interest in being a hatchet man critic who slams everything he writes about. I'll only give a bad review if it's in the public interest, such as a major act releasing a disappointing album. Even then, I'll often keep away.

If I do review, I'll still be completely honest and point out the good and the bad in any release.

I'm primarily reviewing new material only. Each month at Apocalypse Later Music, I review releases from the previous two months. I might stretch a little beyond that for a submission, but not far. Each January, I also try to catch up with highly regarded albums and obvious omissions from the previous year that I didn't get round to at the time. I then bundle my reviews up at the end of a quarter and publish in zine form midway through the following month.

I'm especially interested in studio albums or EPs that do something new and different. I try to review an indie release and a major band each weekday, one rock and one metal, with each week deliberately varied in both genres and countries covered.

If you still want to submit, thank you! You can do so in a couple of ways:

1. Digital copy: please e-mail me at hal@hornsablaze.com a link to where I can download mp3s in 320k. Please include promotional material such as an EPK, high res cover art, etc.
2. Physical: e-mail me for a mailing address.

Either way but especially digitally, please include any promotional material such as a press kit, high res cover art, band photo, etc.

And, whether you submit or not and whether I liked it or not, all the best with your music! Don't quit! The world is a better place because you create.

Submissions of books for review at the Nameless Zine wouldn't come to me directly. If you have books that fit the scope of a predominantly science fiction/fantasy/horror e-zine, please see the contact details at the bottom of the main page at thenamelesszine.org.

I don't review film submissions much any more, as most of my film reviews are for books.

CREATIVE COMMONS

ABOUT HAL C. F. ASTELL

While he still has a day job to pay the bills, Hal C. F. Astell is a teacher by blood and a writer by the grace of the Dread Lord, which gradually transformed him into a film critic. He primarily writes for his own site, Apocalypse Later, but also anyone else who asks nicely. He writes monthly book reviews for the Nameless Zine.

Born and raised in the cold and rain of England half a century ago, he's still learning about the word "heat" many years after moving to Phoenix, Arizona where he lives with his much better half Dee in a house full of critters and oddities, a library with a ghost guard ferret and more cultural artefacts than can comfortably be imagined. And he can imagine quite a lot.

Just in case you care, his favourite film is Peter Jackson's debut, *Bad Taste*; his favourite actor is Warren William; and he believes Carl Theodor Dreyer's *The Passion of Joan of Arc* is the greatest movie ever made.

He reads science fiction, horror and the pulps. He watches anything unusual and much that isn't. He listens to everything except mainstream western pop music. He annoys those around him by talking too much about Guy N. Smith, Doc Savage and the *Friday Rock Show*.

He tries not to go outdoors, but he's usually easy to find at film festivals, conventions and events because he's likely to be the only one there in kilt and forked beard, while his fading English accent is instantly recognisable on podcasts and panels. He hasn't been trepanned yet, but he's friendly and doesn't bite unless asked.

Photo Credit: Dee Astell

My personal site is Dawtrina. I run Smithland, a Guy N. Smith fan site. I founded and co-run the CoKoCon science fiction/fantasy convention. I co-founded the Arizona Penny Dreadfuls. I've run the Awesomelys since 2013. I write for the Nameless Zine.

The Arizona Penny Dreadfuls	azpennydreadfuls.org
The Awesomelys	awesomelys.com
CoKoCon	cokocon.org
Dawtrina	dawtrina.com
The Nameless Zine	thenamelesszine.org
Smithland	guynsmith.rocks

ABOUT APOCALYPSE LATER

Initially, Hal C. F. Astell wrote film reviews for his own reference as he could never remember who the one good actor was in forgettable episodes of long crime film series from the forties. After a year, they became long enough to warrant a dedicated blog.

The name came from an abandoned project in which he was reviewing his way through every movie in the IMDb Top 250 list. Its tentative title was a joke drawn from covering *Apocalypse Now* last and it stuck. It didn't have to be funny.

Gradually he focused on writing at length about the sort of films that most critics don't, such as old films, foreign films, indie films, local films, microbudget films, and so on, always avoiding adverts, syndication and monetised links, not to forget the eye-killing horror of white text on a black background. Let's just get to the content and make it readable.

Four million words later and Apocalypse Later Press was born, in order to publish his first book, cunningly titled *Huh?* It's been followed by half a dozen others with double digits more always in process.

This growth eventually turned into the Apocalypse Later Empire, which continues to sprawl. In addition to film and book reviews, he posts a pair of album reviews each weekday from across the rock/metal spectrum and around the globe. He runs the only dedicated annual genre film festival in Phoenix, Arizona, the Apocalypse Later International Fantastic Film Festival, or ALIFFF. He publishes books by himself and others. He presents programs of quality international short films at conventions across the southwest.

Apocalypse Later celebrated its fifteenth anniversary in 2022.

Apocalypse Later Empire	apocalypselaterempire.com
Apocalypse Later Film	apocalypselaterfilm.com
Apocalypse Later Books	books.apocalypselaterempire.com
Apocalypse Later Music	apocalypselatermusic.com
Apocalypse Later International Fantastic Film Festival	alfilmfest.com
Apocalypse Later Roadshow	roadshow.apocalypselaterempire.com
Apocalypse Later Press	press.apocalypselaterempire.com
Apocalypse Later Now!	apocalypselaternow.blogspot.com
Horns Ablaze	hornsablaze.com

Latest Books from Apocalypse Later Press (available on Amazon):

A Horror Movie Calendar

WTF!? Films You Won't Believe Exist

WTF!?

FILMS YOU WON'T BELIEVE EXIST

WARNING!
*May contain
nuts and other
adult content.*

by award-winning author
HAL C. F. ASTELL

Tempe, Arizona — September 1-4

SCIENCE FICTION & FANTASY CONVENTION

Seanan McGuire
Author Guest of Honor
COKOCON

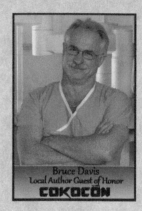

Bruce Davis
Local Author Guest of Honor
COKOCON

Bruce Davis and andyvanoverberghe sponsored by Arizona Fandom
Margaret & Kristoph sponsored by the Phoenix Filk Circle

Margaret Davis
Filk Guest of Honor
COKOCON

andyvanoverberghe
Artist Guest of Honor
COKOCON

Kristoph Klover
Filk Guest of Honor
COKOCON

COKOCON.ORG

2023
COKOCON

Tempe, Arizona   September 1-4

ATTENDANCE WILL BE CAPPED AT 500

LOCATION:
DoubleTree by Hilton Phoenix Tempe
2100 S Priest Dr, Tempe, AZ 85282

MEMBERSHIP:
Adult (12+): $40 (during 2022)
$50 (2023 pre-con) $60 (at con)
Youth (7-12): half current price
Kid-in-Tow (<7): FREE
(limit of 2 per adult member)

HOTEL RATES:
$92 per night (single/double)
$102 (triple) or $112 (quad)

SPONSORED BY CASFS & WESTERNSFA

We're a four day convention over the
Labor Day weekend (September 1-4, 2023).

We host Guests of Honor, an art show,
dealers' room, gaming, filk, room parties, etc.

And, as with all sf/f cons, the heart of the event
is our ConSuite, which all members are welcome
to visit for free food, drink and conversation.

facebook.com/cokocon twitter.com/cokocon1

COKOCON.ORG

Made in the USA
Monee, IL
21 February 2024